COLORING
WITH THREAD

A NO-DRAWING APPROACH TO FREE-MOTION EMBROIDERY

ANN FAHL

C&T PUBLISHING

Text and artwork © 2005 Ann Fahl

Artwork © 2005 C&T Publishing

Publisher: Amy Marson

Editorial Director: Gailen Runge

Acquisitions Editor: Jan Grigsby

Editor: Lynn Koolish

Technical Editors: Franki Kohler and Susan Nelsen

Copyeditor/Proofreader: Wordfirm, Inc.

Cover Designer: Kristy K. Zacharias

Design Director/Book Designer: Kristy K. Zacharias

How-to Photography: Luke Mulks

Illustrations: John Heisch

Production Assistant: Kerry Graham

Published by C&T Publishing, Inc., P.O. Box 1456,
 Lafayette, California 94549

Front cover: *George's Garden* (detail) by Ann Fahl, photo
 by Sharon Risedorph

Back cover: *Button Flowers* by Ann Fahl, photo by Sharon Risedorph;
 George's Garden, by Ann Fahl, photo by Sharon Risedorph

Library of Congress Cataloging-in-Publication Data

Fahl, Ann,

 Coloring with thread : a no-drawing approach to free-motion embroidery /
Ann Fahl.
  p. cm.
 Includes bibliographical references and index.
 ISBN 1-57120-296-X (paper trade)
 1. Embroidery, Machine. I. Title.
 TT772.F34 2005
 746.44'028—dc22
     2004027203

Printed in China

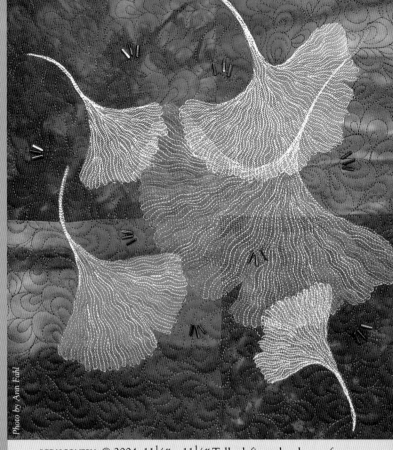
Photo by Ann Fahl

REDISCOVERY, © 2004, 11$\frac{1}{4}$″ × 11$\frac{1}{4}$″ Tulle defines the shape of
the leaf and the variegated thread provides the detail.

ACKNOWLEDGMENTS

Thank you to all my family, friends, and students, and
to the quilters everywhere who have taken time to
share their ideas, time, and inspiration with me. Your
energy, laughter, and friendship have helped me
become the quilter, artist, and author I am today.

CONTENTS

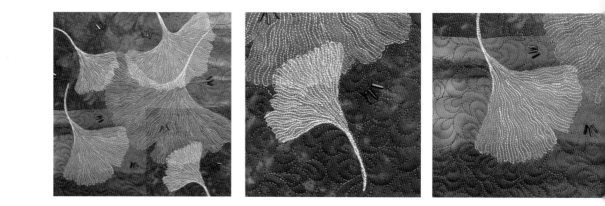

INTRODUCTION

EMBROIDERED GINKGO LEAF, © 2004, 6″ × 6″

This book began in Winona Lake, Indiana, in 1990, when my car wouldn't start. It was Labor Day, and time to leave for home. The car battery had run down, and my uncle hooked it up to the charger and said that in a couple of hours it would be charged up enough to drive home.

At the time, most of my quilts contained leaves. While waiting for my battery to charge, I went out in search of some interesting leaves for a future quilt. That is when I first found the ginkgo trees at the swan pond. They were the most beautiful leaves I had ever seen. As a bonus, they were from my favorite spot in the world!

I appliquéd some of these leaves onto my next quilt. I found that they weren't realistic enough when I outlined them in a satin stitch, so I dropped the feed dogs and covered the surface with free-motion embroidery. That was a life-changing moment! Stitching from the base of the leaf to the outer fanlike edges created beautiful leaves.

The next quilt had ginkgo shapes cut from layers of netting, then stitched with variegated thread. That was all I needed. I've used variegated thread and lowered feed dogs ever since.

It's amazing how things change the course of your life, or the design of your quilts! In this book I've included just about everything I've learned over the years about machine embroidery. This information will help you avoid the first step of having the car trouble, and will give you the benefit of all my experience with thread.

Many people have helped me and supported me in my quilting life. I have found that sharing knowledge with others and asking a lot of questions will help solve problems and improve the quality of your work.

For me, quilting has always been like a treasure hunt. There are lots of trails, ideas, and clues to follow. It's good to be flexible because one idea will always lead to another, which may lead to something unexpected, unplanned, and wonderful.

I never know where I'm going until I get there. Each quilt becomes a new collection of experiences and challenges; that's part of the hunt and discovery. I hope you will enjoy your adventure in the world of free-motion embroidery.

Ann Fahl

WHAT IS MACHINE EMBROIDERY?

 mbroidery is the process of decorating or embellishing the surface of cloth with thread.

Machine embroidery is decorative stitching done with a sewing machine. My definition of machine embroidery is stitching on the fabric, patchwork, appliqué, or other fused elements adorning the quilt top. This is not the same as machine quilting, which is stitching that goes through all three layers of a quilt. Quilting can be seen on the underside of the quilt; embroidery stitches cannot.

Free-motion embroidery is the technique I use most on my quilts. With the feed dogs dropped and a darning foot attached, I control the direction and length of the stitching with my hands. A shape can be covered quickly with thread, adding wonderful texture and detail to an otherwise simple shape. I have fewer problems with thread when stitching

through just the quilt top. Some decorative threads are rather delicate in nature, so stitching through just one or two fused layers results in less thread breakage or shredding than would stitching through the multiple layers of a quilt sandwich.

Machine quilting uses similar techniques, but all the stitching is done through all three layers. This gives a different look to the stitching; there is dimension in the area that is quilted. A machine-embroidered top remains flat. When I quilt a heavily embroidered surface it has a soft dimensional quality that I love.

The following pages contain a gallery of my quilts, followed by a lifetime of information, including background and how-to information. This may seem like more knowledge than you will ever need, but when you are having a problem, this book will come in handy as a reference.

GALLERY

The quilts in this gallery will give you an overview of my work and its development. In 1978, my quilts started as patchwork and hand appliqué. Over the years, inspired by my life and surroundings, I worked to make my quilts more personal. I upgraded my sewing machines and improved my free-motion embroidery skills. This did not happen overnight. In 1988, I declared myself a machine quilter, gave up most handwork, and never looked back! My experimentation with thread began shortly thereafter, bringing a new dimension to my work. In the quilts pictured here, you will find a lot of thread work, including satin stitch, decorative stitches, free-motion using straight and zigzag stitches, and machine quilting.

LEAVES

In my quest to make my quilts more personal, I started to work with leaves from my yard, from the woods in the area, and from Winona Lake. At home, I am surrounded by trees, wildflowers, and animals. I am continually amazed that Mother Nature takes care of all these things and that they thrive without the intervention of man. Having grown up in the city, I thought man planted everything! I want my quilts to celebrate the energy, color, and shapes provided by Mother Nature. These quilts use the ginkgo leaf, because I believe it is the most beautifully shaped leaf in the world. My ginkgo shapes come from two trees by the swan pond at Winona.

Photo by Ann Fahl

GINKGOES ON BLUE AND GREEN, © 2004, 36½″ × 36½″

This was the first time I had ever made a quilt using oversized ginkgoes. My goal was to fill the space with a cluster of leaves that would grab the viewer's attention. Having a hundred little leaves would have appeared cluttered, so I went with just a few that were very large.

Using yellow for the leaves provided contrast to the background as well as creating the focal point of the quilt. To create the illusion of texture, I embroidered the leaves with either a blue or a green variegated thread. The thread choice reflects the color of the background where the leaves are lying and gives the veins a little more punch. They are still yellow, but with more visible detail.

SPRING GINKGOES, © 2004, 33″ × 33″

The colors for the leaves were selected from the colors splashed on the hand-painted background, with the addition of lime green for contrast. I set them inside a fused border to give additional focus to the composition. The leaves themselves were embroidered with variegated thread that blended with the fabric color. For the first time, I tried folding up a few corners of the leaves, allowing the viewer to see a little of the underside of the leaf. This was accomplished by using blue thread on the curled-up segment, contrasting with the embroidery on the top of the leaf.

LARGE BIRDS AND CRANES

Photo by Ann Fahl

One of my fondest memories of my summers at Winona Lake was walking to the swan pond and watching the swans move in the water. Some years they actually had little ones to raise. The swan has become a personal symbol for me—one of peace, grace, and beauty. I started with the swan and later included herons, cranes, and egrets.

CELEBRATION OF LIFE, © 1993, 64½″ × 85″

I consider this quilt to be one of my life-time best. Three whooping cranes are the focal point. My first choice was to use swans, but when I thought about the composition, I decided that birds with long legs were more dramatic. They are standing in front of a red fan for contrast. The idea for the fish to be a platform for the birds came from a greeting card from a family member. Many hours of my childhood were spent fishing. I loved sitting on the end of the pier, watching the bobber and observing the dragonflies flitting around. This entire arrangement is very bold and dramatic because of the bright yellow pieced background of hand-dyed fabrics. The birds were made using a variety of white fabrics, with the addition of turquoise, rose, and gray fabrics to shade each bird.

Photo by Ann Fahl

SYMPHONY OF COLOR I, © 2000, 79¼″ × 55″

As I was making this quilt, I felt it was my life's best. It includes brilliant color and combines all my favorite images and shapes: triangles, water lilies, and swans, surrounded by extravagant amounts of color. When I created the background, I wasn't sure what, if anything, would be put on it; as I worked I just assembled a pleasing array of colors. Later the silhouettes were added using fabric dyed by Laura Wasilowski. Everything is heavily quilted to add lifelike detail. The quilting on the swans was daring for me, as I stitched with a bright, variegated thread in crayon colors. In earlier quilts I always used a matching tone-on-tone variegated thread; this would have been too subtle with all the vibrant color in this piece. I needed something stronger to create the texture on these birds.

FANS

F ans are a beautiful shape. For me they are reminiscent of the shape of the ginkgo leaf, and personally they are another symbol from Winona Lake. They are also perfect for filling with machine stitching. In the early twentieth century, there were Bible conference grounds at Winona. People came from all over the world to hear the music, famous preachers, and orators. The largest building was the tabernacle. It had a dirt floor, windows that opened, and hard wooden benches. Sunday mornings in the summer were unbearable in that building when thousands of people came to worship. The local businessmen realized that there was a potential gold mine in that building. They provided fans, at no charge, for people attending services. One side had a religious scene and the flip side featured the names and addresses of the dairy, mortuary, and other local businesses. During my childhood, these fans were always lying around the cottage. In my opinion, the businessmen were very clever but the fans were ugly. I have kept the idea of the fan and discarded the advertising and the pictures.

Photo by Sharon Risedorph

THREE FANS, © 1996, 35$\frac{1}{2}$″ × 24$\frac{1}{2}$″

The fan shape I used here was new to me. I cut it into pie-shaped wedges to make the fan itself more interesting. I chose two deep-purple cotton fabrics for the fans on either side and an iridescent white semi-sheer fabric in the center. This created a strong visual statement. Using a flat metallic variegated thread and my machine set on zigzag, I embroidered over the iridescent fabric. This created an interesting surface. The other two fans were embroidered with wavy lines and spirals, using a variegated metallic thread for surface interest. The fan motif was repeated again in the background, where blue iridescent seed beads were sewn in a motif that looks like the ribs of a fan.

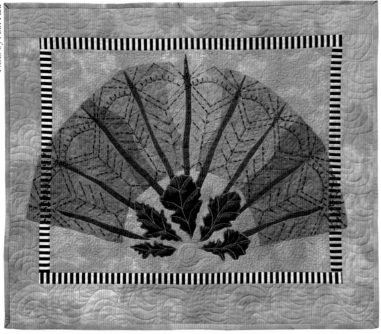

Five green chintz oak leaves left over from an earlier quilt form the base of this fan. Blue strips for the ribs were fused onto the hand-dyed background. Layers of purple, blue, and turquoise tulle were layered in a fan shape to create a background for the embroidery and beads. The tulle was embroidered and held in position using silver thread in a tight spiral pattern. The oak leaves were detailed with satin stitching in silver. A network of bugle beads was stitched over the embroidery. I used several different colors of bugle beads to add some variety to the beading design in the body of the fan. The quilting is simple, using a light blue variegated thread in a meandering design and scallops to add contrast to the fan shape.

BUR OAK FAN, © 1998, $25^{1}/_{2}$″ × $10^{1}/_{2}$″

I thought about this quilt a long time before I ever had time to make it. This is a good creative sign, because it means my brain has already worked out all the details before I begin. When this happens, the quilt almost makes itself! Before fusing the dark red fan onto the background, I cut slits in it to let some of the tan peek through. A printed inner border and a dark red outer border became a frame for the quilt. Three white lilies and green lily pads were fused on top and embroidered. Red bugle beads were scattered in strips to suggest the ribs of a fan, while several layers of thread added shading and detail to the lilies. The background was quilted in a repeated scallop design that contrasts with the embroidery of the flowers. I've found that using a pattern like this, with lots of curves, seems to enhance the subject and create a more interesting background.

RED FAN AND WATER LILIES, © 2000, 23″ × $17^{1}/_{2}$″

SPIRAL ROSES

T he energy of the spiral has always fascinated me. For years I had wanted to incorporate the shape into my work. When I realized that the spirals could be roses or flowers, I was excited by my new idea. They also became perfect vehicles for experimenting with thread.

By the time this quilt was made I had lots of leftover spirals and cutaways from other quilts. My goal was to use some of them in an interesting composition. I used scraps in many shapes and colors, all of which already had fusible web on the wrong side. I made a big discovery while allowing myself to play with the large spirals. Previous spirals had always been machine appliquéd with a satin stitch or a decorative stitch in variegated rayon thread. This time, I used a flat metallic thread and went back and forth over the entire surface, creating a very wide zigzag pattern that literally covered everything. This method was fast, and the thread is very reflective, so it really sparkles when light hits it. So not only did this method save time, but it

looks great too. The little squiggles on the black background were done using a zigzag stitch with the darning foot and variegated thread, after the layers were basted together. This was my first free-motion zigzag, so there were a number of firsts here. Many of these discoveries helped make my next quilt a prizewinner.

This is a perfect example of why it can be interesting to start a quilt with no expectations of what the finished quilt will look like. Begin by arranging scraps or favorite fabrics and see what emerges. Allow yourself to play. When you give yourself permission to do this, all kinds of ideas will float around in your head. Try as many of them as you can.

Photo by Ann Fahl

BROKEN TRELLIS, © 1996, 42″ × 32½″

SPIRAL ROSE GARDEN, © 1997, 62½″ × 82″

This quilt is the culmination of two years of experimentation with the fused spiral motif. This garden is set on a background of 10-inch squares. Notice how the squares transition from bright white at the top to black at the lower edge, creating an interesting movement of color behind the composition. Each rose is machine embroidered with a matching metallic thread in a zigzag embroidery pattern. The leaves and stems are covered with green holographic thread. The metallic and holographic threads add a subtle sparkle to the entire garden. When the quilt is hung on display, it glows as if it has beads covering the surface.

I used spirals that range in size from the little buds to large dinner plate–sized roses. This dramatic range of sizes gives variety to the arrangement and creates a bolder visual statement.

PICTORIAL QUILTS

O ver the years I have felt the need to create story quilts. They become literal interpretations of places and events in the life of my family. These are also fun to make, and they stretch my creativity to find ways to represent unusual objects.

Photo by Mellisa Karlin Mahoney, courtesy of Quilter's Newsletter Magazine

GREAT GRANDMA'S BENCH, © 1995, 38˝ × 35˝

Earlier I mentioned how important Winona Lake, Indiana, is to me and my quilts. This is how I remember the yard during the summer at the cottage. Grandma always made sure there were lots of toys for everyone to play with; you can see a canoe, a motorboat, water skis, beach towels, fishing net, Great-Grandma's flowerpot, and fishing poles. During that very long one-hour wait after lunch before we could go swimming, I liked to make mud pies. So on Great-Grandma's bench you can see all the pails, pans, plates, shovels, and the sprinkling can that I used to create my muddy delicacies. The yard looks cluttered, but it was heaven for me. This was the perfect quilt to experiment in small ways with machine appliqué and free-motion work. Trying out new ideas on a small scale makes the job less intimidating for the novice embroiderer.

SMELLING THE FLOWERS, © 2002, 32½″ × 27½″

Here is Oreo, my cat, sitting on the kitchen ledge, sniffing the pink and white coneflowers that I had just arranged in a vase. I stitched the flower centers with brown thread in a tiny circular pattern, then added another layer of gold thread to give them a realistic two-tone center. In the past I had used only yellow thread on yellow fabric. Wanting to change the colors I normally used forced me to experiment with new colors from Mother Nature. The next problem was that the cat and vase needed a platform under them so they wouldn't just hang in space. I placed a layer of black tulle underneath to create the illusion of a surface and shadow.

This is a true-life scene, and when Oreo jumped down from the ledge, the vase and the flowers were thankfully still in the upright position.

Oreo's back is toward us as she watches the party streamers falling down over her favorite catnip doll and ball. Not only do my Oreo quilts tell a story; they are a challenge to me: I want to see how many body positions I can create for her. The phrase "Happy New Year" is stitched using zigzag free-motion embroidery in heavy black thread over black cotton lettering. The letters appear to be three-dimensional but they are not—this is one of the benefits of zigzag free-motion embroidery. To make the quilt more festive, I used colorful 6-inch squares. I like black and white against the patchwork. Because the cat was to be heavily embroidered, I fused the black and white fabrics on a separate piece of bleached muslin first, did all the embroidery, and then carefully cut her out and fused and stitched her into place. Creating a large embroidery on a separate piece of fabric reduces the possibility of the patchwork being distorted. The big discovery made during the construction of this quilt was that I could create the cat in much less time using a zigzag stitch (which makes a wonderful fur coat) than with a straight stitch. This quilt was started on January 1, 2003, and completed by the end of that same month.

PARTY GIRL, © 2003, 27½″ × 27″

GARDEN QUILTS

F or years I've lived in the woods. Living amidst the trees is wonderful, but until recently the yard and house were always dark in the summer. Now we have lost four very large trees near the house, and at last the sun has found us! I have dug up garden beds on all sides of the house to create more and more room for flowers. The following quilts celebrate the joy I have found in gardening.

Black-eyed Susans are one of my favorite flowers. The ones in my garden were transplanted from Winona. They can really brighten a dark area in the garden. This cluster of flowers is blooming on a background dyed by Robbi Joy Eklow. The day I started this quilt the temperature outside was 100 degrees. I felt the need to work on something that was both hot and cold. I knew the golden color of the petals would look wonderful against the deep blue and purple at the top edge. These flowers are extremely hardy and cannot easily be contained by the edges of the garden, so I designed a border to reflect this. The uneven lines that look like hand stitches help to contain the flowers by framing them, and serve as a border to finish the edge. Actually, I didn't have any more fabric and felt that the quilt needed some type of frame.

Photo by Ann Fahl

LOOKING TOWARD THE SUN, © 1999, 42″ x 34″

The success of an earlier quilt, *White Coneflowers*, inspired me to try to make another prize-winner using black-eyed Susans. To make the quilt more dramatic, I constructed a background of very dark, almost black, fabrics. Knowing that the subject would be yellow and gold, I fused a gold striped inner border in place for the flowers. This created a simple border and repeated the color of the flowers. I cut a big variety of colors and sizes of flower shapes to add interest. To provide the illusion of depth, the blossoms furthest from the viewer are small, and were made using dark gold cotton or gold tulle and then embroidered. Stems were zigzagged in place and the leaves were embroidered with variegated threads. I like combining techniques: the machine appliqué and free-motion work complement each other and provide the viewer with interesting details. Dark iridescent bugle beads were scattered at the base of the plants to add a little sparkle as the viewer walks past.

A BRIGHTER DAY, © 2002, 43½″ × 43½″

Before this quilt was made, all of my work had flowers in full bloom. This quilt changed that pattern. These blossoms are spent, black, and withering. This part of the gardening season saddens me, but it is a part of the life cycle. Some gardeners cut the dead stalks down, but I prefer to leave the remaining stalks alone for the goldfinches and chickadees to snack on in the winter when snow covers the ground. As the designer, I did give my dying flowers a bright autumn background that provides contrast for the silhouettes of the flower stalks. The background is playfully quilted in variegated thread, in a tight meandering pattern or a pebble design at the foundation of the plants. This provides a contrast in texture with the dark subject and a little detail for viewers when they come closer.

END OF THE SEASON, © 2003, 48″ × 48″

Before designing this quilt, I thought about it for a long time. My goal was to combine my two favorite flowers and make them big enough to fill the quilt top. Previously, all my quilts had featured just one type of flower or shape. This time I challenged myself to make the flowers much larger than I had in the past. I wanted to fill the frame to the fullest, so that viewers would feel like they were looking into the flowers. Each flower was heavily embroidered. The coneflower centers were free-motioned with zigzag, blending three or four tones of yellow. The black-eyed Susans were filled with gold and orange thread, and the centers were created with a combination of dark red and brown.

Dimension and shading were added to the leaves by using a layer of black tulle under the embroidery. All these details are important because the viewer is so close to the garden. Iridescent bugle beads were scattered throughout the garden. I love the idea that the slight twinkle of a bead or two on the surface will catch the viewer's attention. Heavy quilting with a dark variegated thread adds texture to the patchwork background. The deep thread color accentuates the shapes and curves of the quilting design. The binding was made from a fabric with wide stripes that incorporates all the colors in the quilt. Most of my quilts use a striped or plaid binding. When cut on the bias, the binding adds a subtle change of pace on the outer edge.

Photo by Sharon Risedorph

AUGUST GARDEN, © 2003, 49″ × 49″

Photo by Sharon Risedorph

GEORGE'S GARDEN, © 2004, 48½″ × 53½″

This quilt was in its early stages when my friend George Hanson died. He was a gentleman of 82 who joined my group of friends for coffee each morning. Over the years he always joked about all the flowers I had given him, so he called his garden "The Ann Fahl Memorial Garden." Now I have a quilt named for him.

This garden of coneflowers and black-eyed Susans is growing on a background of purple squares. As in August Garden, the flowers are oversized to fill up the space inside the fused inner border. My goal in creating this piece was to improve on the composition of that earlier quilt: I started with a rectangle rather than a square, and I wanted my flowers placed closer together. The petals of each flower were embroidered using a straight stitch; the hint of a shadow was created with variegated thread. In earlier quilts, I layered darker threads over the original embroidery to give the illusion of shade; this time I marked where I wanted the shadows to be and filled them in with a darker color. This gave a smoother surface to the flower and saved time too. The flower centers were shaded using several colors of thread and a zigzag stitch similar to that used in the earlier quilt. The piece was heavily quilted in a clamshell design, using dark variegated thread. The outer border quilting was planned and marked ahead of time to include the shapes of coneflowers.

In this quilt, which was designed for a show of art quilts in my hometown, I wanted to have fun with the coneflower idea: deep purple flowers with lime green centers. A hot pink spiral was added for visual excitement and to sculpt the cone-shaped center. The stems are a black-and-white stripe appliquéd with purple and green thread. The leaves finish my crazy garden in shades of orange. After all the embroidery was finished, one additional layer of purple flat metallic thread was added. I love the glitz that just a small amount of this thread adds to the surface. These flowers are far from organically grown, but they were fun to make. The background fabric provided the outlines for the machine quilting. Having made so many "serious" coneflower quilts, I had to make one that was just whimsical.

Photo by Ann Fahl

REALLY PURPLE CONEFLOWERS, © 2004, 28¼″ × 29¾″

WATER LILIES

Taking a boat ride out on Winona Lake was a favorite activity for all the family. My father or his brother could give the best and wildest rides! One of our calmer activities was to take the boat into one of the canals and pick water lilies. There was always a big coffee can in the boat for bailing; we'd fill the can up with the beautiful white flowers, take them home, and put them on the big oak table in the dining room. They are such beautiful, perfect flowers! After they are picked they stay open until evening, then they close forever. In the wild they open up each day. To this day, I feel guilty about having picked all those lilies. Because of the simplicity of their shape they are perfect subjects for lots of thread work. I enjoyed stitching the lily pads in a simple radiating design. I had embroidered several quilts before I realized that lily pads are the same shape as two ginkgo leaves together!

Photo by Ann Fahl

FLOATING IN THE SUN, © 2000, 46½″ × 36″

Three glorious water lilies are blooming on the surface of a sun-filled pond. The flowers vary in color from faded pink to deep rose. My personal challenge in this quilt was to design the lilies so that the viewer could look inside them. The lily nearest to the viewer shows all of its embroidered center, which was perfect for lots of free-motion embroidery. The background was pieced from pastel triangles to create a soft quiltlike environment for the lilies. The lily pads were cut from a mauve and green painted fabric. The veining of the leaves was created using a contrasting variegated thread to give subtle but realistic detail. The quilting bends, twists, and curves around the lilies, adding a waterlike feeling over the surface.

WATER LILIES ON YELLOW, © 2002, 28¼˝ × 28˝

This quilt was part of a group challenge to stretch the creative spirit. I assembled small pieces of yellow fabric and fused them, with raw edges fraying, to a layer of nonwoven interfacing. The border was created using longer strips on the outside edges that are fused into place. Using a four-sided art deco shape, I cut it into lengthwise sections, arranged them in a lily-like shape, and embroidered them onto the fused background. The lily pads were made using one or two layers of purple tulle; this was something I had never done before. They were embroidered into place with spirals of yellow thread, then quilted with a spokelike pattern in purple thread. I love what happens when the tulle lily pads overlap each other, and the transparent floating illusion they give to the quilt. Every small section is covered with thread, either as embroidery or quilting. My creative energies were indeed challenged, from assembling a background of small pieces, to layering and embroidering tulle, to combining the rigid geometric shape of the flower with the soft, natural shape of the lily pads.

WATER LILIES AT SUNSET, © 2003, 25˝ × 32˝

When I was little, I'd watch the sunset over Winona Lake with my great-grandmother. Every evening the family would gather in the yard to watch the color changes in the sky and on the water. For some reason I never liked this quilt. It began with the idea of using the colors at sunset. So I chose bright, rich colors for the silhouettes of the flowers and set them on a yellow chintz background. The quilt hung in an exhibit at a gallery, and when it came back I realized what bothered me. The flowers had no focal point; nothing captured my interest when I looked at them. I stitched fine lines for pistils and stamens, using metallic thread for the extra detail that had been missing. Now I can enjoy these colorful flowers floating at sunset.

Photo by Mellisa Karlin Mahoney, courtesy of Quilter's Newsletter Magazine

THE WALKING BRIDGE, © 2001, 61″ × 80″

Here is the footbridge over the canal at Winona Lake. I've walked over this bridge hundreds of times, and so have my children. We used to throw rocks into the water and enjoy the sound of the pebbles hitting the water and the ripples on the surface. There used to be a mulberry tree nearby, and we could pick and eat a few berries to stain our tongues purple. I made this quilt to celebrate my love of Winona and to feature my glorious embroidered water lilies.

The background was pieced using my free-form patchwork technique. The trees, leaves, and water lilies are heavily embroidered. The lilies are so big that they had to be embroidered first on a separate piece of fabric, then fused into position on the water. I want viewers to feel like they are standing right at the water's edge, looking into my lilies, with my favorite bridge in the background.

GETTING READY

PREPARATION

Lighting

Good light is essential for machine embroidery. Windows that provide natural light are very desirable. If you work at night or have no windows, you need good overhead lighting. I had simple fluorescent fixtures installed on the ceiling and put full-spectrum florescent tubes in them. These lights are available at home improvement stores; they cost more than warm or cool bulbs but are worth the increased expense. Full-spectrum lights give you the ability to see the true colors of the fabrics and threads, whether at night or during the day. They also make it easier for you to see the stitching and all the little details of your work.

Full-spectrum light is also easier on your eyes. If ceiling lighting isn't a possibility, invest in a good lamp that can provide light right over your sewing machine. I also use a clamp-on lamp with a flexible neck, which I can place in front of my machine. I find the clamp-on style preferable to a lamp that rests on the table, because during the process of sewing, a clamp-on lamp can't get knocked off the table.

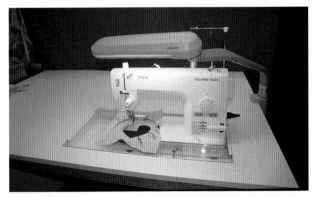

OTT-LITE lamp placed directly above the needle area to increase visibility

Unfortunately, many sewing machine manufacturers place the sewing machine light behind the needle and presser foot instead of in front. This results in a shadow in the working area and reduces the visibility of the stitching path. As we age, we need more light to accomplish tasks than when we were younger, and this shadow becomes more of a problem. Experiment with placement to get maximum lighting with greatest visibility.

Sewing Surface

A large flat surface makes free-motion sewing easier. If your work area is just the bed of the sewing machine, the project will pull away from the back of the machine and will pull and drop at the front and left edge. This will make it harder to move the work freely under the darning foot of the sewing machine. No matter what direction you are stitching, your quilt, pulled by gravity, will always work against you. Various types of bed extenders are available, both from machine manufacturers and other vendors. These extenders are particularly helpful because they create more surface area for the project and are portable.

The ideal solution is to have a large table that the sewing machine sets into, so there is a large flat work surface to support your project. There are many types of machine cabinetry that will give you this flat surface. Check with your machine dealer for tables made to fit your brand.

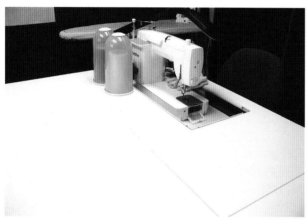

Larger work surfaces make free-motion sewing of any kind easier.

A small machine table can be made larger by clustering smaller folding tables, drop-leaf tables, or gate-leg tables around the back and left edge of the working area. If your work space has to double as an eating area or desk, the tables can be folded up and put away as needed.

A clean work surface is essential. When I'm ready to embroider or quilt, I always find that my sewing table is cluttered with stuff. Take a few minutes to clear away the cat, fat quarters, quilts, extra thread, and other paraphernalia that needs to be removed. Once a large quilt goes under the needle, all these things will get pushed off the edge anyway. Make your life easier and remove all the clutter first.

Sewing Machine Manual

To get the most out of my book, please find your sewing machine manual. Each manufacturer has different ways to change the settings and the tension, different suggestions on how to use monofilament in the bobbin, different darning or quilting feet, and so on. If you don't have the instruction manual, order one from your dealer.

TOOLS AND SUPPLIES

Sewing Machine

The sewing machine is the most important piece of equipment for a person who loves to make quilts. It should become an extension of your arms. My parents got me a new machine when I was in high school; I used it for 25 years. Now I realize that that old machine was holding me back because of all its limitations. If you are using a machine that is more than 10 years old, consider a new one. Ask for one for your birthday, Christmas, or Mother's Day, or go purchase one yourself. Older machines have too many problems to deal with. Stop holding yourself back; trade up to a newer model and make sewing fun again.

When shopping for a machine, start by asking a lot of questions. Not all brands or models of machines can handle free-motion embroidery easily. Choose carefully and be sure to try out the machine before you purchase; it's best to bring your own fabric and thread and try free-motion stitching.

Look for a machine with needle up/down; a clear-view darning foot; and easy-to-adjust tension, stitch length, and stitch width. A knee lift is also a wonderful aid for the machine embroiderer. Most machines come with a throat plate designed to accommodate zigzag stitching. A machine that also has a straight-stitch throat plate (with just a small hole) will make free-motion straight stitches neater. Find a dealer who is willing to spend time with you and who has a repairman who understands free-motion sewing.

If you can't afford a new machine, try a reconditioned top-of-the-line machine from the dealer of your choice. It will improve your stitches and quality of life.

Darning Foot

A darning foot is specifically designed for free-motion work. The design differs with each manufacturer. Usually the foot has a round or oval base and is mounted on a flexible or spring attachment that allows the foot to move up and down with the motion of the needle. Check your machine manual or ask your dealer for the type suitable for your machine. If the standard darning foot for your brand of machine isn't to your liking, ask about alternatives or try some of the generic feet on the market.

Test the darning foot. Can you easily see where you are going? This is important when stitching around appliquéd shapes and embellishments. The larger the foot, the more visibility you have. Some styles have an open design in the front. This increases visibility, but the open toe can get tangled in the seams, stitches, or embellishments. I've found one that has a large oval metal rim with a clear plastic insert in the center. It is designed specifically for straight stitching and gives excellent visibility and good control over the fabric layers being stitched.

Another good option is a spring darning foot with a clear plastic oval. This foot provides good visibility and can be used for straight or zigzag free-motion stitching.

Assortment of darning feet

Scissors

A good assortment of scissors is always helpful to the sewer. A small pair of scissors with bent or curved blades makes it easier to trim threads in the stitching area or in the embroidery hoop. These scissors also have the added advantage of being safer to use; you are less likely to snip into the surface of your work by accident. One accidental snip, and the top of your quilt will have a hole in it. These scissors are indispensable.

Double-curve scissors are more versatile. They make it easy to trim threads while your work is still in the hoop, and you can also trim out seam allowances with them.

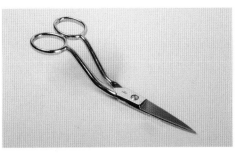
Double-curve scissors

Curved-tip scissors are helpful for snipping threads at the surface of the quilt safely when working with or without a hoop.

Curved-tip scissors

If you have large hands, you might find large-handled appliqué scissors more comfortable. There are many kinds of scissors available; try as many as possible to find the pair that fits your needs.

Iron

An iron that provides large quantities of steam is essential when there is a lot of embroidery. Steam relaxes the stitches and bobbin thread, allowing the fabric to be worked back into its original shape. Remember that steam irons have a rather short life. If they don't hit the floor first, or get knocked over by the cat, I usually have to replace mine every three years or so.

Steam iron

Hoops and Stabilizers

You'll need a machine embroidery hoop and stabilizers for free-motion work.

Hoops

There are two types of embroidery hoops: wooden or plastic. Wooden hoops have a metal screw for tightening, and plastic hoops have an inner metal clamp. Both types are modestly priced, and they each have their strong points. Hoops in general are particularly helpful for beginners, as they keep your work taut and give you something to hold onto.

Hoops keep the work taut.

Stabilizers

When you are doing lots of stitching, the fabric can become distorted. Placing a layer of stabilizer underneath will help keep the embroidery pucker-free and flat. Stabilizers can be purchased by the yard or in various packaged quantities.

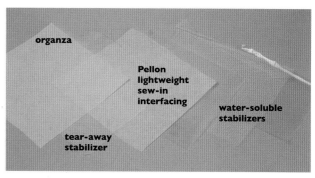

Stabilizers help keep stitches from puckering.

For a beginner, I recommend using the clamp-type embroidery hoop with the addition of a tear-away stabilizer, nylon net, or nonwoven interfacing. Try all the stabilizers as you perfect your technique. Several stabilizers are suggested for each small study (starting on page 66) so you can try different ones and decide which you prefer. The more experience you have, the better you will understand how to adjust the sewing machine. Experienced embroiderers need only use a hoop or a stabilizer for most areas. The goal is to cover the area with thread while keeping the area as flat and soft as possible.

HOOPS

ADVANTAGES	TYPE	DISADVANTAGES
■ Inexpensive ■ Holds work firmly	**HOOP WITH TIGHTENING SCREW**	■ Awkward to move hoop from one area to another while under the needle. ■ Inner rim needs to be wrapped with cotton twill tape to help grip hooped fabric.
■ Inexpensive ■ Easy to move while under the needle	**HOOP WITH INNER METAL CLAMP**	■ Metal inner clamp sometimes snaps out of position. ■ Difficult to put clamp in place when the work is thick with layers of embroidery or fabric.

STABILIZERS

ADVANTAGES	STABILIZER	DISADVANTAGES
■ Thread work remains soft, no stiffness ■ Nothing to remove on the back of embroidery	**MACHINE EMBROIDERY HOOP**	■ Difficult to embroider large areas ■ Thread draw-up a problem, depending on bobbin thread choice*
■ Easily removed by gently tearing away from the back ■ Inexpensive ■ Minimal draw-up*	**TEAR-AWAY STABILIZER** (looks like paper or nonwoven interfacing)	■ Removal sometimes breaks the stitching ■ Adds paperlike stiffness to embroidered area ■ Only the outside edges can be removed
■ Lightweight ■ Doesn't add stiffness to embroidery as tear-away does ■ Helpful when embroidery is through one layer (not over a fused shape)	**WATER-SOLUBLE STABILIZER** (looks like plastic sheeting)	■ Expensive ■ Can't use steam to press thread work before removal ■ Need to immerse embroidered fabric in water to dissolve; if not completely rinsed out, fabric becomes stiff
■ Inexpensive ■ Easy to find ■ Lightweight ■ Minimal draw-up* ■ Soft hand to finished embroidery	**NYLON NET** (this is the inexpensive netting with large holes, not the softer tulle)	■ Has to be trimmed away from back with scissors
■ Lightweight ■ Minimal draw-up* ■ Soft hand to embroidery	**ORGANZA**	■ More costly ■ Has to be trimmed away from back ■ Not as available as other products
■ Lightweight ■ Soft hand to embroidery ■ Easy to find ■ Moderately priced	**NONWOVEN INTERFACING, LIGHTWEIGHT (SEW-IN TYPE)**	■ Has to be trimmed away from the back with scissors

*Draw-up occurs when stitching distorts the surface of the fabric. Heavy embroidery can curl or shrivel up the fabric, causing puckering. Stabilizers help control draw-up; for a more thorough discussion, see pages 41 and 48.

THE FUSING PROCESS

In my quilts I fuse fabric shapes onto the surface to create my designs. These shapes give me a second layer of fabric to add crispness to the embroidery and to create stronger color in the design.

It is wise to start each large project with fresh paper-backed fusible web; I prefer to use regular-weight Wonder-Under.

I find that the product changes over time. My philosophy is: if the web of glue is separating from the paper, don't buy it, and resist using old product at home. I purchase *only* what I can use in a month or two. Humid summers are hard on the product, so buy less at a time if you live in a humid climate.

How to Fuse

1. Draw a shape on paper.

Draw or trace shape on paper.

2. Darken the line with a heavy felt-tip marker so the design is easier to see through the fusible web.

Darken drawing with heavy felt-tip marker.

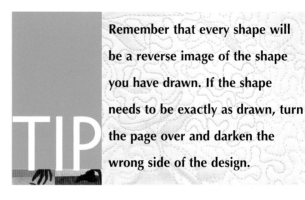

TIP Remember that every shape will be a reverse image of the shape you have drawn. If the shape needs to be exactly as drawn, turn the page over and darken the wrong side of the design.

3. Lay paper-backed fusible web over the shape (paper side up) and use a pencil to trace the design on the paper side.

Trace shape onto paper side of fusible web.

TIP Because the paper-backed fusible web is lightweight and you can see through it, move it around until it is perfectly placed on just the right part of the fabric.

4. Roughly cut along the outside edges of the design. Leave extra paper around the pencil line.

Cut around outside of design.

5. Place the fusible web (paper side up) on the wrong side of the selected fabric and press in place using a *dry* iron. Leave the iron briefly on the paper—just a second or two (or as instructed on the directions that come with the fusible web).

Press on wrong side with dry iron.

6. Cut out the shape exactly on the lines.

Cut shape exactly on drawn lines.

7. Peel off the paper.

Peel off paper backing.

TIP

If the paper doesn't want to peel off, let the fabric and fusible web cool, then try the following:

While holding the shape, rub your thumbnail on the edge of the paper side or take a pin and scratch a deep line or an × in the center of the shape. Then try peeling off the paper.

If you are going to use old product, always test it first. Old product is very difficult to peel, and it is better to throw it out rather than have a specially cut shape fray because the paper was difficult to remove.

8. Place the fused shape on the background fabric and pin it in place.

9. When the design or arrangement of shapes is final, press in place using steam, holding the iron on each area for about 10 seconds. Remove the pins as you come to them. Please consult the directions on the package for pressing time. Some brands differ.

Press in place with iron on steam setting.

When you are fusing, the iron will inevitably get some sticky stuff on it. A quick way to remove the glue is to place a scrap of cotton batting on the edge of the ironing board. Using pressure, wipe the hot iron on the edge. Continue to move the iron until you no longer see black residue. You can also clean the tip and the sides of the soleplate this way. This will mostly eliminate the need for chemical iron cleaners.

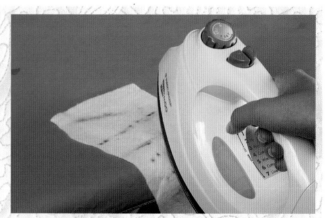

Rub hot iron over cotton batting to remove excess fusible web.

If you should get some of the black fusible glue on the top of the quilt, try using a soft clean pencil eraser, moving it with the grain of the fabric to remove small smudges.

FREE-MOTION EMBROIDERY ESSENTIALS

This chapter includes detailed information about thread, bobbins, and machine needles. This material will become a valuable reference for you. The more you know about the tools of free-motion embroidery, the easier it will be to solve problems as they arise. In other words, when you have a problem, you'll be glad this information is here!

THREAD

Using Thread

Early in my sewing life I was a fabric person. I loved all the colors and the softness and texture of yard goods. In my quilts I mix commercial fabrics with hand-dyed and painted yardage. My thread work becomes the texture and detail that can be seen when the viewer comes up close.

In the early 1990s, when I first became aware of the many varieties of thread available, a new world

opened up to me. A person can collect hundreds of spools of thread and they will fit in one grocery bag. So storage is less of a problem than for fabric! Collect all the colors and varieties that you find appealing.

With so many kinds of thread on the market now, you need a way to organize your collection. I use a wheeled plastic cabinet with five drawers. Each drawer contains one type of thread, sorted by color. Keep your thread types separate so you don't accidentally use a decorative thread for mending clothing.

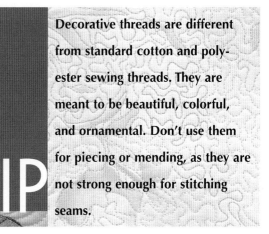

TIP Decorative threads are different from standard cotton and polyester sewing threads. They are meant to be beautiful, colorful, and ornamental. Don't use them for piecing or mending, as they are not strong enough for stitching seams.

There are so many beautiful threads available to quilters today. The variety offers us an unlimited number of choices that can change the appearance of the quilt surface. When first starting to sew with some of these threads, you may get frustrated with thread shredding or breakage. Don't give up! The information in this book will give you tips on how to avoid these problems by making adjustments on your sewing machine.

Designing With Thread

From an artistic standpoint, I divide decorative thread into two categories: solid color and variegated. Variegated thread can be just one hue, changing from light to dark, or it can change from color to color. My first choice when embroidering is a solid color thread or a one-hue variegation. For machine quilting I always prefer variegated thread of any type. Whatever you decide to use is a matter of personal choice and color availability.

The Thread Test

How do you know which thread is right for your project? Select several possibilities. Unroll about 36 inches of each and let the thread puddle on the fabric. Usually one will speak to you and say, "I'm the right one." If this doesn't happen, use the thread to sew small tests on a scrap of matching fabric. Hold it up to the quilt and see if you like the effect. This may seem a little time consuming, but it is much less time consuming than hours of ripping out stitching. It can take two or three hours to rip out fifteen minutes of free-motion machine embroidery!

Auditioning thread puddles

TYPES OF THREAD FOR MACHINE EMBROIDERY

Cotton

Cotton is a natural fiber that has been around for centuries. Many quilters prefer 100% cotton thread for their piecing, appliqué, embroidery, and quilting. Long-staple cotton is the most desirable. It has a subtle luster and is quite strong, so it is able to withstand heavy use and washing. Cotton thread is available in many weights and in a huge variety of colors and variegations that are appropriate for embroidery, quilting, piecing, and appliqué.

Cotton thread

Polyester

Polyester is a man-made fiber that creates a strong thread. It comes in a range of colors, from subtle to brilliant, and in solid, neon, and variegated. It can have a dull, cottonlike finish (spun polyester) or it can have a very shiny surface that imitates silk or decorative rayon (trilobal polyester). There are a great number of new color choices and variegations in this category.

Polyester thread

Rayon

Rayon thread is made from cellulose and is considered a natural fiber. It imitates the luster of silk and is available in a beautiful array of colors and variegations. This type of thread is best used only for decorative stitching. It isn't a strong thread, so it is not suitable for use in clothing or quilt construction. It does provide a beautiful line of stitching on the surface of fabric. It is the perfect choice for topstitching, embroidery, or quilting.

Rayon thread

Metallic

Twisted metallic thread

Metallic threads have been around for many years. In ancient times they were actually fine wires of gold, silver, and copper. Fortunately for us, technology has made more affordable, washable, and flexible threads that imitate these precious metals and that can be woven or used for embellishment. The fiber content of metallic threads can vary. For the most part, the fibers are polyester or a polyester and nylon blend. They can also be twisted with rayon. Metallic thread comes in two basic types:

Twisted metallic thread behaves much like traditional sewing thread when used in the machine. Several plies or strands of yarn are twisted together. This gives the thread strength and allows it to move through the tension system of the sewing machine without causing too many problems. The thread provides a moderate amount of sparkle or reflection of light in the stitching.

Flat metallic thread is the most reflective thread on the market. It is made by slicing a thin sheet of coated polyester into thread widths before it is wrapped on spools. It comes in solid, holographic, and variegated forms. This shiny thread can add interesting effects to the surface of the embroidery like no other thread. At times, this thread can truly *challenge* the artist and the sewing machine! Be careful when pressing this thread; some kinds will easily melt and disappear. Always test a small sample first to see if a pressing cloth is necessary. One additional caution: do not stitch over or across this thread. When the needle pierces it, the thread can break and result in rough ends. So if you choose to use this thread, make sure it is the *last* layer sewn.

Flat metallic thread

Silk

Silk is a natural fiber that comes from the silkworm. It is the most lustrous and costly thread on the market. The colors range from rich in tone to very soft and subtle. When using silk thread, take care to anchor the ends of your stitching; it likes to come undone.

Silk thread

Monofilament

Monofilament thread

Monofilament thread is the workhorse of machine quilting. It is feared by some and revered by others. It is available as 100% nylon or 100% polyester. It is quite strong, even though it is .004mm in size. When used correctly, it is invaluable. Be careful when ironing because some brands are quite heat sensitive (nylon more than polyester). Monofilament has an undesirable shine if the wrong thread "color" is selected. Use clear monofilament on whites, pastels, and medium hues, and use the smoke on dark colors. This thread can be used for quilting in seamlines (in-the-ditch) and around appliqués and embroidery. It can also be used in the bobbin for free-motion embroidery. However it is used, it is almost invisible. This thread is so fine that you can get miles and miles of it in the bobbin. For people who do heavy machine work, this is a bonus.

When monofilament thread was first introduced to the home sewing market, it was considerably heavier than it is today. If you tried it in the early 1980s and made a bed quilt with it, the little ends were so stiff that you would think someone was sticking you with a pin! Most of us said, "I'll never use that stuff again." But give monofilament another try; the finer, flexible thread today is much easier to use and softer to the touch.

In the thread industry today, there are continuing efforts to improve monofilament thread. One brand has a delustered nylon monofilament available in clear and smoke. Another brand has a polyester thread with less stretch and heat sensitivity. Continue trying the new products to find out which ones work best for you.

Testing a New Type of Thread

Every time you purchase a new type of thread, it is wise to make a test sample. This will give you the opportunity to see how the thread stitches, as well as learning how to set your machine to best use the thread. Use the chart on page 46 to keep your notes, and be sure to keep your stitched samples.

1. Try stitching using a straight stitch with standard tension and the feed dogs up. The stitches should be balanced, without the top thread peeking through to the underside or the bobbin thread pulling to the top. Usually only the top tension will need to be adjusted. Make a note of the tension setting and needle used. Your goal should be to stitch with the thread so that there is no puckering or looping of thread visible on the top or bobbin side of the fabric.

2. Now try a zigzag stitch with a tear-away stabilizer underneath. It may be necessary to loosen the top tension a little to prevent the bobbin thread from peeking up through the top. For embroidery, it is acceptable for the top thread to slightly show on the underside. Note your machine settings.

3. Try the thread with monofilament in the bobbin. Note the settings.

4. Use bobbin thread in the bobbin. Note the settings. (See pages 40–41 for more on bobbin thread.)

5. Lower the feed dogs and try straight stitching free-motion style. Use an embroidery hoop or a tear-away stabilizer underneath. Note the settings.

6. Lastly, try free-motion zigzag stitching with a hoop or stabilizer. Note the settings.

TOP THREE THREAD TIPS

You will undoubtedly encounter some problems when trying new types of threads. Don't become frustrated. **The top three ways to deal with thread trouble are as follows:**

1. Change the tension. With decorative thread, loosening is necessary. Loosen or lower the tension setting by one number, test, and keep lowering the tension by one number at a time until the shredding or breaking stops.

2. Try a new needle. Do you need a larger size? Is your needle damaged? (See pages 44–46 for more on needles.)

3. Remove the top thread and the bobbin completely, then re-thread. Decorative threads are slippery, and when you aren't looking they can slip out of the tension disks or plates and cause trouble. Sometimes they will unwind in the bobbin case and cause problems in the bobbin area.

It is very important to make notes of what settings were successful for the type of thread used. In the future you can refer to your notes and make the appropriate adjustments. In time, these adjustments will become automatic when you change threads, and all the steps listed above won't be necessary. But for now they will help you learn to adjust your machine.

Thread Sizing

When talking about thread size, the *smaller* the number, the *thicker* the thread. Most thread, but not all, is labeled with the size designation. Thread weight is the number that indicates the thickness or heaviness of a thread. This is actually a combination of length and weight. To help you remember how thread sizing works, remember the following: if 40 kilometers of thread weigh 1 kilogram, it is a 40-weight thread. If 50 kilometers of thread weigh 1 kilogram, it is a 50-weight thread. When the thread is thinner or finer, there is more yardage, hence the higher number. Threads purchased for general sewing use are labeled 40-weight (sometimes written as 40 wt.). This is the size you are familiar with and have used for general sewing and patchwork.

Understanding thread sizes is important because thread size will affect the amount of time and stitching it will take to cover a fused shape with thread. It will take longer to cover a shape with a 50-weight thread than with a 40-weight thread. A 30-weight will fill faster but will result in a coarser finished product.

ANN'S TIPS FOR THREAD SUCCESS

I give the following tips to all my students to help them solve thread-related problems.

1. Always test the thread and the machine stitch desired on a scrap of fabric *before* working on the actual quilt.

2. Use Schmetz top-stitch needles in your machine to reduce friction at the eye of the needle.

3. Experiment with the bobbin thread in your machine. Try regular-weight sewing thread, monofilament, or fine bobbin thread to improve the stitch.

4. Reduce the machine tension by gradually loosening it one number at a time.

5. Threads are designed to unwind from the spool in different ways: cross-wound thread should be placed on a horizontal spool pin; parallel-wound thread should be placed on a vertical spool pin. When you are experiencing difficulties, try switching the spool to a horizontal or vertical position. If your machine has only one spool pin, find an adaptor that will allow the spool to sit in the other position.

Parallel and cross-wound thread

6. If the machine skips stitches, try moving the needle position as far to the left as possible.

7. Use a silicone product on the spool of thread to prevent skipped stitches. One brand name is Sewers Aid. Put a thin line of the product along the length

of the spool and reapply as needed. **Before using this product, check with your machine dealer to be sure it is appropriate for your model. Apply this liquid after you have exhausted all other possibilities!**

8. When using metallic thread, stitch more slowly than normal. Apply silicone liberally to the spool. (Again, be sure to check with your machine dealer before using a silicone product.)

9. Your choice of fabric also influences the ease of machine stitching. Soft cottons are easy to work with. Very firmly woven fabrics, including chintz, will cause thread breakage as a result of friction and heat built up during stitching.

10. When you near the end of a spool, the thread will begin to pull or kink. Change the position of the spool to either vertical or horizontal, or wind the remaining amount of thread onto a bobbin and place the bobbin on the spool holder on top of the machine.

11. Use a thread stand.

12. If the thread is twisting and knotting through the tension system, put a thread net over the spool or cone.

Thread net prevents thread from twisting and knotting.

Thread stand allows thread to feed evenly.

13. When all the stitching is complete, press the stitches so they are flat. This will give more sheen to the thread. *Test press* a sample before applying lots of heat or pressure to your embroidery project, because some threads are heat sensitive.

14. If you are using a Bernina sewing machine (or a machine with a similar bobbin case), put the bobbin thread through the little hole in the finger of the bobbin case. This adds extra tension on the thread and is helpful when the thread is an extra-fine bobbin thread or monofilament. It helps balance the stitch without having to actually tighten the tension on the bobbin case.

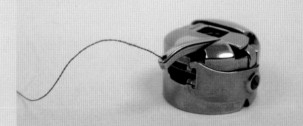

Put thread through hole.

15. If the sewing machine is computer controlled, turn it off for 10 seconds to let it reset itself.

16. Check the power supply. If you are using a power strip or surge protector, check to see how old it is. It may not be giving you a consistent power supply. The fuse may need to be replaced. This can be a mysterious and difficult problem to solve, especially at workshops.

17. When everything is going wrong and you've tried all the other options, try a different type of thread. That way you can rule out the possibility of having a bad spool of thread.

18. Get to know the sewing machine manual. Do you know where it is?

19. Take notes on what is successful for each type of thread and stitch. You can refer to these notes later when you need to use the same combination again.

20. See the Troubleshooting Guide on pages 91–94.

21. Still having problems? Take a walk, pet the cat, or do something else for a while before tackling the problem again.

22. If you have tried all the above and you're still having problems, take your machine in for servicing. Explain that you are doing free-motion embroidery and take a sample showing the problem.

BOBBINS

The Bobbin Case

No one talks much about the bobbin case, but this little round object is in charge of half of every stitch made by the machine! We need to pay more attention to it. Clean it out, brush it out, and oil the case as directed by your machine dealer.

Bobbin cases

All sewing machines have a bobbin case; some are removable and some are the drop-in type. As you become proficient in machine embroidery, it will be helpful to have a second bobbin case. This way one bobbin case can keep the factory settings. The second can be loosened or tightened, depending on the type of thread you choose. Mark the second bobbin case with a dab of red nail polish or permanent black marker to differentiate it from the factory case. This will ensure that you will be able to sew using factory-set equipment for regular sewing when your feed dogs are up.

If your machine has a drop-in bobbin rather than a removable bobbin case, check with your dealer to see if a second bobbin case is available for your machine.

Bobbin Thread

40-weight cotton or cotton blend thread has been used in the bobbin since the sewing machine was invented. This can be a little too heavy to use in free-motion embroidery.

Cotton bobbin thread is much finer and more yardage will fit on the bobbin. It is more appropriate for free-motion work.

Monofilament is wonderful because so much thread will fit on a bobbin. Experiment with both the polyester and the nylon monofilament threads. Some machine brands do not tolerate this thread well or prefer one fiber over the other.

Polyester bobbin thread is a new product on the market. It is quite strong and smooth. It is 60-weight and quite a bit will fit on a bobbin. It also comes in a wide array of colors.

Bobbin fill thread

Prewound bobbins are a nifty little convenience for machine embroiderers. The really fine thread is wrapped very tightly onto a cardboard or plastic bobbin. Unfortunately, because they are made in generic sizes they sometimes cause problems in some brands of machines. If you are experiencing problems in the bobbin, this might be the reason. Replace it with a bobbin you wind yourself and see if that solves the difficulty. The color selection of cotton bobbins is limited; the polyester bobbins come in a wide range of colors.

Prewound bobbins

Draw-up: Notice puckering around edge of shape.

If you are using prewound bobbins with cardboard sides and are having problems with the bobbin, carefully remove the cardboard sides and put the bobbin back into the machine.

TIP

Bobbin Problems

There are two bobbin problems, **draw-up** and **peek-through**, that can be solved by proper adjustment.

Thread draw-up occurs during free-motion stitching. The fabric becomes distorted when it is stitched in many directions. When the hoop or stabilizer is removed, the stitched area tends to shrink or draw up as the thread relaxes. This effect can be reduced by steaming the area *immediately* after it is removed from the hoop, or before the stabilizer is removed.

If the rippling is severe, you may need to loosen the bobbin tension, top tension, or both. Another possible cause could be too much tension on the thread while it is being wound on the bobbin. Try winding the bobbin more slowly or bypass one of the thread guides to reduce the amount of stretching that is taking place. (See page 48 for more on draw-up.)

Peek-through is my term for the little dots of bobbin color that pop up between the stitches, or the little loop of thread that pulls up from the bottom when you change stitching directions. First try loosening the top tension a little. If that doesn't work, then the bobbin tension needs to be tightened. Turn the slot in the bobbin case to the right, or clockwise, just slightly to tighten. Test the stitch on a scrap and continue making small adjustments until the color stops peeking through.

If you are using one color in the bobbin and a different color on top, this will continue to be a problem. Peek-through will be reduced if the bobbin color is changed to match the top thread or the fabric being embroidered.

Peek-through: Notice dots of color.

Adjusting Bobbin Tension

If you want to adjust the bobbin tension, please consider purchasing an extra bobbin case before doing this. That way you can have one case set at the factory setting and one to experiment with.

When I discovered polyester bobbin thread, my world changed. It is great in the bobbin for embroidery or quilting. I did have to tighten my bobbin tension, which is something your home economics teacher probably told you never to do. Check your machine manual to locate the tiny screw that regulates bobbin tension. With a tiny dot of permanent marker, mark where the slot on the head of the screw is pointed. With a small screwdriver, turn right to tighten or left to loosen the bobbin tension.

Picture the screw as the face of a clock. To tighten, if the slot is set at 12:00, move it to 1:00 and test the stitches. If that isn't enough, tighten to the next hour, and so on. Continue to tighten one hour at a time until the thread stops pulling up to the top. My bobbin case tension was set at 11:00 and I had to tighten my case to 2:00.

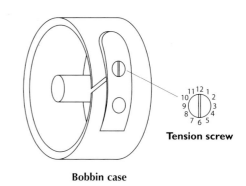

Tension screw

Bobbin case

Here's another way to check the bobbin tension. There should be some resistance when you pull the bobbin thread through the case. If it comes out easily, tighten it until you feel more tension.

Why do you need to tighten the bobbin tension? Because bobbin thread is so fine and smooth that it can be easily pulled to the top side when you change directions. To balance the stitch to accommodate this new thread, the bobbin needs to be tightened so the thread can't be pulled to the top as easily.

If your machine has a drop-in bobbin, there is still a way to tighten or loosen the bobbin tension. Look in the owner's manual to see where the little screw is located. Turn it to the right to tighten and to the left to loosen.

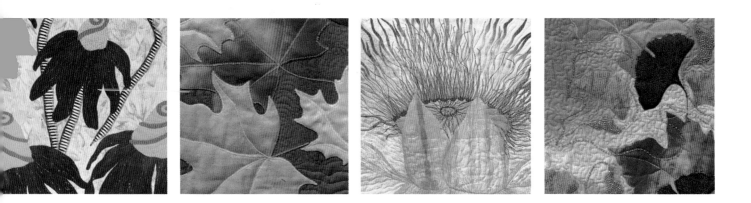

BOBBIN THREAD SELECTION CHART

ADVANTAGES	THREAD	DISADVANTAGES
■ Remains unseen on many different colors ■ No color peek-through ■ Lightweight for heavy thread work such as satin stitch ■ Large quantity of thread will fit on bobbin ■ No lint buildup in bobbin area ■ If used in the bobbin when quilting, this will give you the best-looking quilt back	**MONOFILAMENT**	■ Stretches; considerable amount of draw-up with heavy free-motion embroidery ■ Heat sensitive; nylon more sensitive than polyester ■ Must use press cloth if pressing on wrong side ■ Unsightly sheen to the line of stitching if wrong "color" used, even when used in the bobbin ■ Not the best choice for bed quilts; nylon thread has been known to get cloudy with use and washing
■ Natural fiber ■ No heat sensitivity ■ Wide range of colors ■ Minimal draw-up ■ Gives a soft hand to quilt ■ Washable	**COTTON (40-WEIGHT)**	■ Makes embroidered areas thick and heavy with thread ■ Starts and stops are very visible if used for quilting ■ Must continually fill new bobbins ■ Color may peek through to right side ■ Lint buildup in bobbin area
■ Finer thread, more yardage in bobbin ■ No heat sensitivity	**COTTON BOBBIN FILL**	■ Color choices are limited ■ Color may peek through to right side ■ Lint in the bobbin area
■ Smooth, strong thread ■ Large quantity of thread in bobbin ■ Wide color choice ■ Lightweight ■ Minimal draw-up ■ Great with rayon and metallic decorative threads ■ Colorfast when washed	**POLYESTER BOBBIN FILL**	■ Minor heat sensitivity ■ Minor color peek-through ■ Starts and stops are visible on back when used for quilting ■ Must tighten bobbin tension

Monofilament in the Bobbin

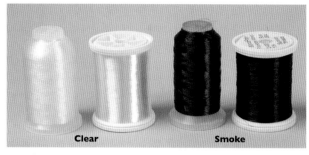

Monofilament for the bobbin

Should you use nylon or polyester monofilament? They are both strong and fine threads. Some people prefer one type over the other. Purchase a spool of each and see which you and your sewing machine like best. Both are man-made fibers and have similar attributes.

Here's what you need to know about using monofilament in the bobbin.

Use the clear when sewing on white, pastel, or medium hues. Use the smoke when sewing with dark colors. If in doubt, make a little test on a scrap of fabric and see which one you prefer.

When winding a bobbin, be cautious and follow the machine manufacturer's directions. Remember that this thread does stretch and it is quite strong. As you are winding, fill the bobbin no more than ⅔ full. The pressure on the center and the sides of the bobbin can be considerable. If it is stretched too tight, sometimes you can't remove the bobbin from the winding pin. If the bobbin is old or the plastic is getting brittle it can break under the tension. On the plastic bobbins you will notice tiny hairline fractures growing out from the center hole. Eventually this cracks and the side pops off, allowing all the thread to pop off and you have a tangled mass of thread. Before winding your bobbin hold it up to the light and see if there are any signs of stress. If the bobbin is metal, the top and bottom can be pushed out of alignment.

Rotate the bobbins you use for monofilament. Check them for imperfections before winding. Throw them out if you suspect any problems. This way you won't fill them by accident later.

If you take the above precautions with the bobbin, there should be few problems. Yet I hear people say they should wind the bobbins very slowly on the machine. Some people have even told me they wind monofilament by hand! If I had to do this, I'd never stitch with it. Fill the bobbins using a modest speed on your machine and you should be alright. If you experience problems with filling them, contact your dealer to see if there is a special system you should be using for your brand of sewing machine.

When quilting with monofilament in the bobbin I sometimes use clear in the top with smoke in the bobbin, or the reverse. It depends on what looks best with the backing fabric you've chosen. In my opinion the best-looking quilt backs are made by stitching with monofilament. This is because no thread color is visible on the underside of the quilt. Only the texture is visible. Places where you have started and stopped or retraced a line are not obvious as they are with all other thread. This is particularly important when a quilt is to be judged.

SEWING MACHINE NEEDLES

Buying sewing machine needles is as exciting as buying a set of new tires for your car. You already had four old ones; now you have new ones. But the tire is what actually makes contact with the road, and having good tires is essential for your safety, just as having the proper needles is essential for successful machine embroidery.

Needle Basics

Using the wrong needle is one of the biggest problems beginners have when experimenting at home.

To make life more interesting, the needle sizing system is just the opposite of thread sizing. The larger the number, the larger the eye and the thicker the needle. A 70/10 is very thin and pierces a tiny hole in the fabric. A 110/18 is a very heavy needle for sewing on blue jeans. The first number is the European size; the second is the American sizing system. Usually both are printed on the package.

The needle in your machine is small, so its importance is often overlooked; but this is the part that actually makes the stitch! There are a number of brands available on the market. To the naked eye, they may look the same, but they aren't. Save yourself a lot of aggravation; buy the highest-quality brand that your sewing machine dealer recommends. It is worth the extra money.

The differences between the types of needles are very small, yet these differences make a big difference in your ability to be successful as an embroiderer.

Needles with a bigger or longer groove in the blade provide more protection for the thread, resulting in less shredding and breakage.

A deeper scarf on the back side of the needle means it is easier for the hook (in the bobbin area) to complete the stitch. This means fewer missed or skipped stitches.

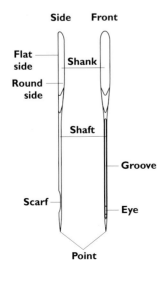

A bigger eye means less friction, heat, and abrasion. This results in less thread breakage. The tip of the needle should be sharp and undamaged. Needles with a damaged tip, whether bent, dull, or burred, will damage the fabric. Notice the difference in the eyes of the universal and embroidery/top-stitch needles.

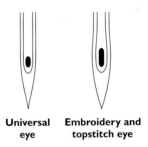

Universal eye   **Embroidery and topstitch eye**

Types of Machine Needles

There are many different types of needles. There are highly specialized needles made for every use and type of machine. As a quilter you are most likely to have or need the following four types:

A **universal** needle has a sharp tip that will pierce a tiny hole in the fabric. This is generally the type of needle needed for piecing and clothing construction.

An **embroidery** needle has a larger eye with a groove and a deep scarf. This groove will protect the decorative threads when piercing all the layers.

A **metallic** needle has a large eye and a large groove to reduce shredding of the metallic thread.

A **top-stitch** needle is ideal for sewing with all decorative threads. This type of needle has a larger eye than the others, a long channel or groove above the eye, and a sharp point. When the needle is piercing the fabric, the thread will nestle or rest in this groove, which reduces the amount of friction and heat built up at the eye of the needle. Friction is what causes the thread to shred and eventually break, resulting in frustrated sewers! Take advantage of my thousands of hours of experience, frustration, and tears—use top-stitch needles when embroidering.

In order to simplify my life and reduce the number of products on hand, I limit the needles I purchase to universal and top-stitch.

So what size do you choose? Here's a guide:

- 70/10 universal needle for monofilament thread
- 75/11 universal needle for piecing and garment construction
- 75/11 or 80/12 topstitch needle for most rayon or polyester decorative threads
- 90/14 topstitch needle for decorative threads that are a little heavier, or that shred when using the 80/12
- 100/16 topstitch needle for the very heavy metallic twisted #20 threads

These choices work for me. Keep notes on the needles that work best for you.

Problems With Needles

After hours of continuous stitching, the tips of the needles get dull and the metal surface is no longer shiny. If you placed a worn needle under a microscope, you could see that the surface actually gets corroded and pitted. When you notice that the needle doesn't pierce the fabric easily, it means it's time to replace the needle.

Replacing the Needle

- When you start a new project, start with a new needle.
- If you hit a pin or bead while you sew, a burr or rough edge will start to snag or pull the fabric. Replace the needle.
- If you have hit something, the needle may also bend. For safety, replace it as soon as you notice it.
- It is possible that a new needle right out of the package is defective. The chances are less if you use high-quality needles. If there are problems with a new needle, replace it.
- Always ask your machine dealer what brand of needles to use. I found out that some cheaper brands are microscopically longer, and this can result in problems with delicate machine timing.

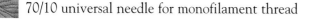

THREAD NOTES

Thread type	Needle type	Tension settings	Fabric	Bobbin thread	Stitch type (Decorative?)	Stitch length	Stitch width

FREE-MOTION EMBROIDERY

When I purchased a new machine, the new computer machine wasn't capable of making the subtle width changes in satin zigzag stitching that I had been doing. So, I needed to find another way of stitching my leaves in place. To overcome this, I decided to lower my feed dogs and try stitching free-motion. Free-motion embroidery added texture and realistic detail to my leaves that I had never achieved before. As an added bonus, free-motion stitching was faster than sewing around the outside edges of every leaf with a satin stitch. Let's stop talking about free-motion and get started.

GETTING STARTED

Trimming Seam Allowances

When you are embroidering on a patchwork background, the seam allowances can add unwanted bulk to embroidered areas. The complete seam allowance can be trimmed away from the wrong side of the fused appliqué, so the seams will not show through to the top when pressed, and thick layers will be eliminated when stitching. *Always trim away just before the area is embroidered.*

1. Mark both edges of the fused shape with straight pins.

Mark edges of fused shape with pins.

2. Turn to the wrong side and carefully trim away the seam allowance between the pins.

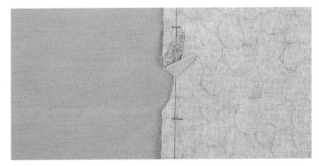

Turn work over and carefully cut away seam allowance between pins.

3. Immediately begin the embroidery over the recently removed seam.

Using a Hoop

Free-motion embroidery is the method I now use to cover all my fused appliqué. For a beginner it is best done in a hoop made specifically for machine embroidery. (See page 28 for more on hoops.) This will give you something to hold onto while embroidering.

To insert your work into a hoop, place the shape to be embroidered in the center of the plastic rim, then squeeze the handles on the metal band and press down so it snaps into place. The hoop keeps the work taut, so there is less puckering or draw-up.

Avoiding Draw-Up

What is **draw-up**? During the free-motion process the base fabric is pulled this way and that with lots of machine stitching, and the fabric wants to shrink or curl up under the stress of the stitches. This can occur if the machine tension is too tight. Another cause may be that the yarns in the fabric actually compress under the stress of the embroidery. The embroidery hoop provides some stability to the fabric, so draw-up is less likely to occur. Before removing the work from the hoop, make sure the iron is hot and steaming, so the embroidered fabric can be steamed the instant it comes out of the hoop. This will heat set the stitches and base fabric into position. If the embroidery still draws up, try a layer of lightweight stabilizer under the area in addition to using a hoop. If this still doesn't solve the problem, loosen the bobbin tension.

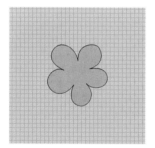

Threads in base fabric before embroidery

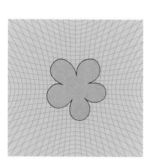

Yarns in the fabric become compressed and distorted during embroidery.

Embroidering

Prepare the Embroidery

1. Fuse the shape to be embroidered onto the background fabric (see pages 30–32 for more on fusing) and center it in the hoop.

2. Replace the standard sewing foot with the darning foot (see page 27 for more on darning feet).

3. Thread the machine with decorative thread and use bobbin fill or monofilament in the bobbin (see pages 33–39 for more on thread).

4. Lower the feed dogs. If you don't know how to lower the feed dogs, check the owner's manual for your sewing machine.

5. Set the machine for straight stitch.

6. Embroider a test sample in the hoop without any stabilizer. If the work shrinks up too much, you can add a layer of stabilizer underneath. Finally you are ready to begin!

Embroider

1. Position the hoop under the needle.

2. Put the needle down into the edge of the fused shape and then back up, pulling the bobbin thread up through the top surface.

3. Hold both threads to the rear of the darning foot and begin to sew (moving the hoop slowly) in a straight or curved line.

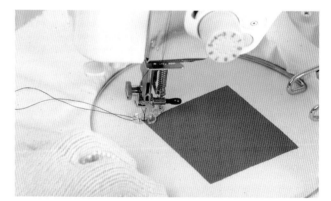

Pull threads to top and back before stitching.

4. Move the hoop from side to side slowly with your hands. The machine should be sewing rather fast. Remember that the feed dogs have been lowered, so they no longer control stitch length. You must lightly hold the edge of the hoop and move it to control the stitches. A *side-to-side* motion is preferable to a front-to-back motion because it is easier to see what needs to be stitched next.

5. Check your work. The key to free-motion embroidery is to control the hoop by moving it slowly with your hands while your machine is running fast. This doesn't sound right, but it works. If you find your lines of stitching looking jagged, it's because you need to speed up your machine.

To embroider effectively, completely cover the fused shape with stitches. I cover the shape with slightly wavy lines of stitching, making sure all the edges are sealed with thread. Curvy lines are easier to make and have more eye appeal than straight lines. Mother Nature doesn't make straight lines, so why should you?

Move with side-to-side motion, stitching wavy lines.

When placing work in the hoop, check to make sure the corners of the project are not folded under the hoop or in the area to be embroidered. Nothing is worse than accidentally stitching the corners of the project to the underside and having to cut the project to remove the hoop.

6. Make sure the stitching actually goes over the edge of the appliquéd shape before turning around and stitching back in the other direction. This seals the raw edges in place and reduces the amount of

raveling. When stitching near the edge of the fused shape, slow down, then stop just when you go over the edge. Take one or two stitches up or down alongside the edge, then return in the opposite direction. With free-motion embroidery there is no need to zigzag the edges of each shape because they will eventually be covered with thread.

Stitching over edge

Finish the Embroidery

1. When the shape is covered with thread, leave it in the hoop while you heat the iron.

2. Make sure the iron is hot and steaming, then remove the work from the hoop and steam it *immediately* from the top or right side. This will set the stitches in place and reduce the amount of draw-up.

3. If the project draws up after the steaming, the next time you stitch gradually loosen the top tension on your machine (one number at a time) until you get less puckering. You may loosen it all the way to zero if necessary. If this isn't enough, place an additional piece of tear-away stabilizer under the area to add extra firmness, in addition to the hoop.

Before you begin stitching each day, or anytime you have changed the thread or bobbin, test the stitch on a scrap of fabric before you begin.

PRACTICE EXERCISES

 ow is your chance to sit down at your machine and try this technique on some scraps of fabric.

Free-Motion Exercise #1: Getting Started

This exercise is just to play and feel the freedom of motion that you've never had when the feed dogs were up.

1. Cut out 6 squares 2″ × 2″ and fuse them on a contrasting piece of fabric.

2. Place the fabric in a hoop. Rehoop as necessary.

3. Use a matching color of thread to entirely cover the first square with lines of stitching. Make sure the edges of the shape are covered.

4. On the second square, stitch in one direction, then add another layer of stitching going in the opposite direction.

TIP When using a hoop, hold the plastic rim lightly with both hands. Avoid holding the metal handles.

5. Cover the third square with a variegated thread.

6. Cover the fourth square with a wavy line of stitching instead of a straight line. You will find this easier.

7. Cover the fifth with tiny spirals like the center of a flower.

8. Try another color of thread on the remaining square.

9. Try writing your name in script. If you are having fun, doodle around the edges. Fill up all the space around the squares with doodling.

Exercise #1

TIP Remember to have your machine stitching fast and move your hands and hoop slowly.

To be successful, you must have good control with your hands and be able to diagnose problems that arise with the thread and machine stitching. Lots of practice will give you physical control. Knowing your machine and reading all the information on thread and bobbins in this book will help solve problems. If you are experiencing problems—thread breakage, loops, stitch skipping, shredding, and so on—refer to the Top Three Thread Tips on page 37 and Troubleshooting on pages 91–94.

Take a Break

Take a few minutes to do something else every 20–30 minutes. Your eyes will get tired and your arms and shoulders will get tense if you concentrate at the machine for too long. Get up and walk around. If your hands get tired, try using quilter's gloves.

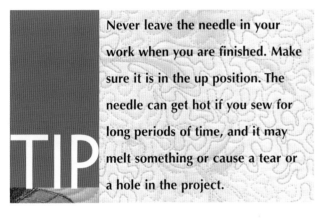

TIP Never leave the needle in your work when you are finished. Make sure it is in the up position. The needle can get hot if you sew for long periods of time, and it may melt something or cause a tear or a hole in the project.

Free-Motion Exercise #2: More Practice

1. Cut out and fuse 3 leaf or petal shapes onto a larger piece of contrasting fabric.

2. Place the fabric in a hoop. Rehoop as necessary.

3. On the first shape, use a contrasting color thread. Stitch down the center to the farthest tip, then back to where you started. Keep going back and forth until the leaf is filled.

4. On the second leaf shape, stitch straight down the center with a slightly curved line. Now fill in with more lines of stitching going at an angle to simulate the veins in a leaf. It may seem a little awkward at first, but by the time you fill up the leaf it will be easier.

5. Try it again.

The leaf on the right demonstrates inadequate thread coverage of the shape. The stitching doesn't completely cover the raw edge. Over time, the edges will curl up and begin to fray.

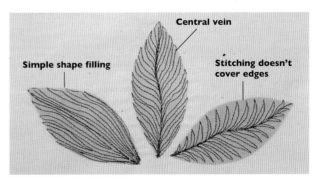

Simple shape filling **Central vein** **Stitching doesn't cover edges**

Exercise #2

It is possible to cover any shape with as much thread as you like. The shape may be densely covered with many layers or lightly covered so the fabric underneath shows through. Your decision depends on your skill level, the shape, and the amount of texture or detail desired.

FREE-MOTION ZIGZAG

The same free-motion techniques can be used with a zigzag stitch set to a medium width. This stitch is perfect for covering an area quickly. It is also a good way to make fur on a cat or a dog, centers of flowers, text, or anything you want to be a solid mass of thread. The lines of stitching are less directional in appearance than the straight stitch we've already discussed. Zigzag adds an overall texture. There are numerous uses for free-motion zigzag. If you draw a single line with the zigzag, it's like writing with an old-fashioned fountain pen. The width changes when the direction is changed.

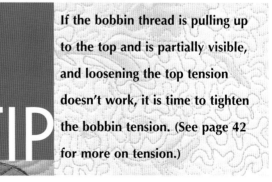

TIP You must sew slower with the zigzag free-motion stitch. Move the work from front to back, rather than the side-to-side method used for straight stitches.

You may find it necessary to lower the top tension on the machine for zigzag stitching. Lower it one step at a time and test on a scrap first.

Be sure to use a throat plate and darning foot that accommodate zigzag stitches.

Free-Motion Exercise #3: Zigzag

1. Cut out a 2″ × 2″ square and fuse it to a piece of background fabric.

2. Place the fabric in a hoop.

3. Experiment with the zigzag free-motion stitch. See how the look of the stitch changes when you move the fabric in a side-to-side motion rather than from front to back? Fill the square completely with thread. Now pivot the square and stitch in the same manner, this time crossing the original stitching. With some shapes, you may find it easiest to go around the outline of the shape first, then fill in the center in one direction, and then cover up any thin spots by sewing in another direction. Overlap the lines of stitching and the shape will appear more opaque.

Start.  Pivot and start again.

Exercise #3

TIP If the bobbin thread is pulling up to the top and is partially visible, and loosening the top tension doesn't work, it is time to tighten the bobbin tension. (See page 42 for more on tension.)

Free-Motion Exercise #4: More Zigzag

1. Cut out and fuse a leaf shape to a piece of background fabric. (You can use the same piece of fabric from Exercise #3.)

2. Place the fabric in a hoop. Because of the nature of the zigzag stitch, draw-up is more of a problem than it is with a straight stitch. As a beginner, you may find it helpful to use both a hoop and a layer of stabilizer underneath.

3. Fill the leaf shape with zigzag free-motion embroidery. Compare it to the leaf in Exercise #2 and see how different it looks from the straight-stitched one. Try the zigzag stitches with contrasting thread, too. Another option is to cover a shape with two directions of stitching as seen in the example below.

4. Try writing and doodling around the shapes. Notice how the stitch changes when the direction is changed or the hand movement is slowed down or speeded up. The more you play with this technique, the more uses you will find for it. Experiment with changing the width of the stitch. Make a note of the widths you prefer.

Exercise #4

Free-Motion Exercise #5: Color Blending With Zigzag

Blended layers of different-colored threads can add shading and the appearance of volume. To successfully blend colors, determine the direction of the light source as you plan your stitching. Start with the lightest color along the lighted edge and cover ¼ to ⅓ of the area with thread. Next, change thread to the next darker color. Cover more of the shape with thread, slightly overlapping the lighter thread. Continue to add layers of new thread colors, getting darker until the entire shape is filled.

1. Cut out and fuse a small oval shape on a piece of background fabric.

2. Place the fabric in a hoop.

3. Choose 3 colors of thread that blend from light to dark.

4. Divide the oval into three units.

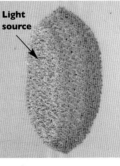

Divide the oval.   Exercise #5

5. The first color used should cover a larger area to allow for the overlap of the second color. For each color of thread, outline the area first, go back and forth to cover the area, and then go back a second time in the opposite direction to fill in the gaps.

6. Each color unit should slightly overlap the one next to it. If you are not satisfied with the blending of the thread, zigzag the area again until you achieve the look you want.

ENDING THE STITCHING

The ends of the thread must be secured by either:

- Backstitching
- Stitching in place
- Using the machine's automatic lock-off stitch (use only when the feed dogs are engaged)
- Pulling the ends to the back side, then knotting and clipping
- Ending on an outside edge that will be covered with additional thread work

It is quite important that the ends of the thread be secured in some way. This is especially critical if you are constructing clothing or a quilt that will be subjected to wear or washing. Plan to finish stitching where it will be crossed or covered with another layer of embroidery or quilting stitches. This is more assurance that your ends will not come undone.

EMBROIDERING LARGE AREAS

Filling up large spaces with embroidery poses several challenges for the machine embroiderer.

- The more stitching there is, the more possibility for draw-up to occur. This will distort the size and shape of the quilt top.
- Large embroidery will not fit in the hoop.
- Embroidering over a tear-away stabilizer makes the quilt very stiff, almost like cardboard.

Fortunately, I have found a way to work around these problems.

If you are going to embroider an extremely large flower, for example, I would suggest fusing the flower elements onto a piece of lightweight muslin. Divide the embroidery into hoop-sized sections. When the embroidery is finished in the hoop, steam it the instant it comes out of the hoop. Then move the hoop to the next section. Continue embroidering and steaming until the design is complete, with all the colors and details necessary. Despite all the steaming and pressing, you will notice that the fabric is quite distorted. Pin the fabric onto a dressmaker's cutting board. Block the finished piece as instructed on page 56.

You can iron paper-backed fusible web on the back of the large embroidery. Then *carefully* cut out the flower, cutting as few threads possible, and fuse it onto the new background. Use matching thread and lightly free-motion stitch the shape onto the quilt top.

You may want to use a stabilizer under this large area when stitching the shape in place. The tear-away products are much too stiff for use in large areas, but they work well for satin stitching and stabilizing small embroidered areas where the majority of the product can be removed.

When the stitching is heavy, I have found that either nylon net or a lightweight sew-in nonwoven interfacing works the best. (See pages 28–29 for more on stabilizers.) The finished embroidery will be softer with either of these choices underneath.

EMBROIDERING MEDIUM-SIZED AREAS

If the shapes to be embroidered are not so big that it is necessary to create them separately as above, they can be embroidered right on the background in the same manner as small shapes. Here's how:

1. If the embroidery is to be done over a patchwork background, trim away all the seam allowances behind the fused subject. This should be done just before the embroidery begins. (See page 47 for more on trimming seam allowances.)

2. Mark the stitching lines on the fused shape with a pencil.

3. Place one layer of lightweight nonwoven interfacing under the background fabric where you will be stitching.

4. Use safety pins to hold lightweight interfacing in place. Straight pins will work, but you may find that you are continually getting jabbed with the pins.

5. Insert the project in a hoop.

6. Stitch one small area at a time, then remove the hoop to steam the area. Replace the project in the hoop for the next area to be filled. Continue stitching, steaming, and moving the hoop until the entire subject is covered.

7. Trim away the excess interfacing.

8. Block the entire project when finished, as described on pages 56–57.

FREE-MOTION STITCHING WITH METALLIC THREAD

I like to think that metallic thread is the icing on the cake. You can try it out on any of the exercises in this chapter. Some machines handle metallics easily; others are severely challenged by them. When layering several types of thread, use the metallics, particularly the flat ones, as a *last* step. They can split or break if you do any additional stitching on top of them, especially when using a larger needle. So, just like the icing, this is the very last layer on the cake.

TIP

When using metallics, always stitch more slowly, use a 90/14 top-stitch needle, lower the top tension on the machine, apply Sewers Aid (if needed), and use the metallics as the last layer.

LETTERING ON QUILTS

When text is needed on a quilt, try this:

1. Use a computer to print the text in very large-sized (125- to 150-point) fonts.

2. Turn the paper over and darken the outline of the text.

3. Trace the backward text onto the paper side of fusible web.

4. Iron the fusible web to the wrong side of the selected fabric.

5. Use small, sharp scissors to cut out the letters.

6. Arrange the letters on the quilt and fuse them in place.

7. Place a layer of crisp tear-away stabilizer under the area to be stitched and free-motion zigzag, filling the shapes very carefully.

8. Steam well, then remove the excess stabilizer.

LAST WORDS ON FREE-MOTION WORK

Practice. It takes time to learn how to free-motion embroider effectively. The more you practice and experiment, the better your skill level will become. There will be some aspects that you enjoy and some that you do not.

It has taken me what seems like a lifetime to polish up my free-motion skills. Do not give up when you get frustrated. Take some time off, and then try again using scrap materials until your confidence improves. Experiment with every type of thread you've collected. Take notes on what works and what does not.

When you feel more confident in your free-motion work, plan a project that is small. All the studies included in this book are small and are designed to give you a variety of skills and ideas that create wonderful effects on the surface of fabric.

FINISHING THE EMBROIDERY

FINISHING AND FINAL PRESSING

All your hard work creating a machine-embroidered piece can be ruined if you skip this very important step: blocking. Having been a hand knitter since kindergarten, I knew that a sweater looked much better when it was steamed into shape. The same goes for a quilt.

Every time you embroider on fabric, surface distortion takes place. The stitching goes in many directions and pulls the yarns in the fabric. By steaming the piece, it can be forced or pulled back into its original shape.

Blocking the Embroidery

The supplies you need for blocking are as follows:

 A long straight-edge ruler or carpenter's metal measuring tape

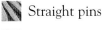 Dressmaker's cutting board (cardboard with grid printed on it, 40″ × 72″)

 Straight pins

 Steam iron

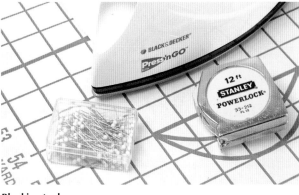

Blocking tools

1. **Pin.** Line up the bottom edge of the project on a line in the grid. Use straight pins to pin the edge of the block or quilt onto the grid every 3 to 4 inches, or as needed. (Insert pins so that the tips are aimed at the middle of the quilt and the heads are angled away from the center.) Next pin the right edge. Pull and smooth the left side into position and pin. The top edge is the hardest to get into line if the project is heavily embroidered. Pull, tug, and smooth into place as best you can and pin as often as needed.

Pin project to cutting board for blocking.

2. **Steam.** Set the iron to a steam setting. Steam the block or quilt while it is pinned onto the cardboard. Let the iron **hover** above the surface. **Do not use any pressure**; you do not want to flatten the piece, just straighten it. Let it dry completely. If there is still distortion on the edges, steam and pull or push the problem area with your hands until the project is square again. Re-pin and steam again. Trimming the edges of the project should only be done as a last resort.

3. **Remove pins.** Take out the pins when the fabric has cooled and dried.

This is absolutely the best way to make a top absolutely square. The printed grid is a big help in lining up the edges while the steam relaxes the fibers into the desired shape.

Blocking the Quilt

The blocking process should also be repeated after the top has been quilted. Machine quilting distorts the piece just as embroidery does. This time, you will need the carpenter's metal measuring tape to use as a guide. The batting and backing extend beyond the quilt top, so it is difficult to use the lines printed on the board. Hook the end of the measuring tape on one edge of the cutting board and pin or lock the other end. Now use the metal edge as a guide to pin the edges of the quilt top in place, just like you did before. Steam heavily with the iron, taking care not to press down on the surface.

After the quilt sandwich has been blocked, cooled, and dried, remove the pins and trim off all the excess batting and backing with scissors or a rotary cutter. This will give you the straightest edges to bind that you've ever had.

If the quilt is too large for one cutting board, butt two to four together on the floor or on a tabletop. Pin, steam, and let dry as above. This process may not be fun, but it will give you a straight, square, professional-looking project.

Judges are impressed by quilts that hang or lie flat. They look very professional. Whether you want to sell your work, compete in shows, or just be proud of your finished product, block your work. It is time well spent.

TIP

A quilt can be blocked at many stages:

- **When patchwork blocks are completed**
- **Before a border is sewn around the patchwork**
- **After the border is applied**
- **After the embroidery**
- **After machine quilting**
- **After packing and shipping; if a quilt is heavily creased during shipping or storage, stretch it out and steam it heavily**

Use edge of carpenter's metal measuring rule as guide.

TIPS AND REFINEMENTS

The following information is an accumulation of tips, thoughts, and wisdom from my years of quiltmaking.

Safety

Take care to make sure all thread clippings are disposed of. Thread, particularly monofilament, can wrap around tiny fingers and toes; it can be swallowed and become a danger to small children and pets. At my sewing table, I always have two small wastebaskets, one on either side, so I can easily throw out all strands of thread. Thread can be dangerous if swallowed.

On a related issue, never leave a hand-sewing needle threaded, either in a pincushion or on a table. Your pet might try to pick it up in its mouth and swallow it.

Projects With Many Spools of Thread

I've made quilts with as many as 50 different spools of thread. You may find it helpful to have a bowl or basket near the sewing machine to hold all the different colors of threads you have used in a project. Store them in this container until the quilt is completely finished. That way, if you need to go back and find a particular color of thread, you only have to look through the bowl instead of your entire collection of thread and guess what spool it might have been.

Keep the thread in a basket or bowl until the quilt is finished.

Clean Up the Edges

After the embroidery, there will be some little ends and ravelings that need to be trimmed away. This is a very simple process if you have a little pair of sharp scissors. Simply fold the embroidery so the fraying edges are standing straight up. Now you can carefully trim off all those little hairs. Folding right on the edge of the fused shape is the key. This also works for machine appliqué.

Fold embroidery to make fraying edges easy to trim.

Clean Up the Back

When using a stabilizer, regularly tear or cut it away. If pieces are left on the wrong side, they may catch on the throat plate or the table edge, making it difficult to smoothly move your project back and forth.

Clean and Oil the Machine

Learn how to clean and oil your machine—it needs to be done on a regular basis to keep the machine in top shape. Check with your dealer to find out how often this should be done. Some machines require little to no oiling. Others need it after every eight to ten hours of sewing. Find out which type you have and learn how to do this right by following the instructions in the machine manual.

Before oiling, be sure to remove all the lint in the bobbin case and around the feed dogs. Check with your dealer on recommended cleaning procedures. Some recommend using a brush provided by the manufacturer; others recommend using canned air to blow out the lint. Cleaning and oiling are simple tasks that will keep your machine running smoothly.

Cleaning Spots on Your Quilt or Embroidery

One of the hazards of working at the machine is the possibility of getting a spot on your project. Somehow, I think these spots magically appear, but it could be machine oil, food, or something a child or pet has deposited on your work. After you have spent hours on your quilt, this can be devastating.

A nifty product from S.C. Johnson can really save your project. It is called SHOUT wipes. They are packaged in a little box that can be found in the laundry section of your grocery store. There are twelve little packets inside; each contains one moist towelette that can be used to remove spots and stains from your work. Keep one or two near your machine, one with your workshop supplies, and a few in your purse. The directions are on the package. I gently rub the towelette in tiny circles on the stained area until it gets foamy. When the spot is gone, I take a dry towel or tissue and blot the excess moisture. The company recommends washing, but I prefer to wipe the area again with fresh water and blot the excess with a dry cloth.

SHOUT wipes are a handy product for removing small spots and stains on your project.

Change Your Mind?

After the embroidery is finished, and you decide that the flower should be red instead of blue, you can make that change!

1. Trace the flower, making it larger than the original. Remember to reverse the image when tracing onto the paper side of the fusible web.

2. Fuse the shape to your choice of new fabric and cut it out.

3. Iron the new flower onto a lightweight piece of fabric.

4. Embroider as desired.

5. When the embroidery is complete, iron a layer of paper-backed fusible web to the back of the stitched fabric and carefully cut out the new flower.

6. Fuse the new flower over the original flower and lightly free-motion embroider over the edges to camouflage the old flower underneath.

The key to success is to make sure the new shape is large enough to cover the old embroidery. Now you have a flower that is the right color, without having to rip the old one out!

Quilting Machine-Embroidered Areas

For quilting I use monofilament thread both on top and in the bobbin for stitching around **all** machine-embroidered shapes. Because the thread is so fine, it virtually disappears when used around the heavier decorative threads. The initial machine quilting is done to secure the layers together. I stitch in vertical seamlines about every 4 to 6 inches. Then I outline all the embroidered areas to give them dimension. If the embroidery is large, I then also stitch right on top of the embroidery to hold it in place. For example, if I'm working on a leaf, I will first stitch around the leaf, then quilt down the center vein and the auxiliary veins as well. This will give the piece realistic dimension. You may also quilt over the veins with a contrasting color to create more visual interest.

After the outlining is complete, I fill in all the empty spaces of the quilt with quilting designs, using a decorative thread on top and monofilament on the bottom. When the quilt is finished it is really loaded with thread! Remember to block the piece before sewing on the binding. (See pages 56–57 for more on blocking.) For more information on machine quilting, see Resources on page 96.

Doing Thread Work After Layers Are Basted

It is easier to do really heavy thread work through just the top layer. This causes less stress on the threads, and all the messy ends are hidden on the inside. But you can do the thread work after a quilt sandwich is basted. Keep in mind that when heavy thread work is done through all three layers of the quilt, the layers become flat. If the stitching is light, it creates a pleasant amount of dimension on the surface. The real downside is that all the thread work on the back can be quite messy. This isn't a problem if the quilt will be hanging on a wall, but the finished piece will not hold up well in competition, where judges closely examine the workmanship.

When you finish a quilt, there will always be an area or two where you would like to add more stitching and color, so go ahead. Be careful to pull the threads up to the top and hold them behind the darning foot so they don't get tangled up below. Keep stitching until you are satisfied.

  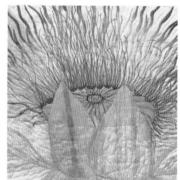 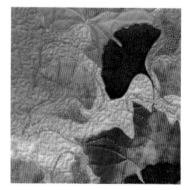

STUDENT GALLERY

All of the work found in this Student Gallery was created by students who have taken my Garden Design and Embroidery Workshop. During the multi-day class, each student designs and fuses a quilt top. Then they learn and practice the free-motion embroidery techniques that you are learning in this book.

Photo by Sharon Risedorph

GINKGOES, 11¼″ × 11¼″, by Franki Kohler, Oakland, CA

Photo by Sharon Risedorph

READY FOR THE PIE II, 25″ × 31″, by Sally Morris, Walnut Creek, CA

LOAFING IN THE LUPINE, $31\frac{1}{2}'' \times 17\frac{1}{2}''$, by Jaxine Andersen, Juneau, AK

DOGWOOD IN SPRING, $28'' \times 28''$, by Marion Gotschall, Juneau, AK

JAPANESE IRIS, $27\frac{3}{8}'' \times 32\frac{5}{8}''$, by Marilyn Fisher, Hillsboro, OR

POPPIES (inspired by a painting by Annette Kieser), 28″ × 28″, by Gen Nester, Juneau, AK

FROM THE COTTAGE DOOR, 32¼″ × 27″, by Jeanne Pfister, Kaukauna, WI

PROJECTS

BRANCH OF LEAVES, 9″ × 9″

BRANCH OF LEAVES

In this project you will practice filling small spaces and creating heavy lines with thread.

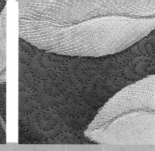

SUPPLIES

See pages 26–40 for a complete description of supplies.

FABRIC

- 1 square 6″ × 6″ of solid or mottled fabric for the center

- 2 squares 6″ × 6″ of a blending or contrasting fabric for the corners

- 1 square 6″ × 6″ of fabric for the leaves

- Fabric for the backing and binding

- Batting

THREAD

- Thread to match the background for piecing

- 40-weight decorative thread: 1 solid color for the leaves, 1 solid color for the stems

- Bobbin thread

STABILIZERS

- 1 square 8″ × 8″ of nylon net, tear-away stabilizer, or organza as a stabilizer

- 1 rectangle 2″ × 7″ of tear-away stabilizer for the stems

- 1 square 6″ × 6″ of paper-backed fusible web

INSTRUCTIONS

Make the Background

1. Cut both corner squares diagonally once to create 4 triangles.

Cut diagonally once.

2. Center the long diagonal side of 2 triangles on opposite sides of the center square, right sides together. Sew using a ¼″ seam.

Sew triangles to opposite sides of center square.

3. Press the seams toward the corner triangles.

4. Attach 2 more triangles on the remaining sides. Press.

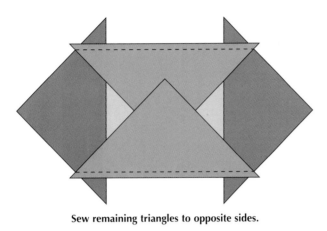

Sew remaining triangles to opposite sides.

Prepare the Appliqué

See pages 30–32 for a complete description of fusing techniques.

1. Trace 7 leaf shapes onto paper-backed fusible web and fuse them to the wrong side of the leaf fabric. Use the leaf pattern on the next page.

2. With a pencil, lightly draw a curved line for the main stem.

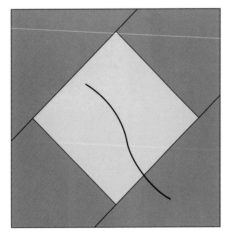

Lightly draw pencil line for stem.

3. Cut out the leaves from the fused fabric. The leaf at the end of the branch can be trimmed a little smaller.

4. Remove the paper backing and place each leaf about ⅛˝ away from the penciled stem.

Remove paper backing and place leaves.

5. Press the leaves in place using steam.

6. Use a pencil to draw a slightly curved line down the center of each leaf.

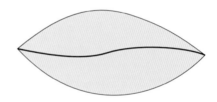

Lightly draw curved pencil line down center of each leaf.

Embroider

See pages 47–49 for a complete description of free-motion embroidery techniques.

1. Place the prepared project on top of your choice of stabilizer and secure in an embroidery hoop. Lower the feed dogs, thread the machine with the leaf color thread, and set the machine for straight stitch.

2. Start at the base of a leaf and move the fabric slowly back and forth, covering the leaf from the drawn center vein to the outside edge. Make sure the stitching line goes completely over the outside edge of the leaf.

3. Move from side to side. Head toward the tip of the leaf, then turn around and move down the remaining half. Secure the ends as discussed on page 54.

Start.

Move up to tip, allowing stitching line to curve, then down remaining side.

4. If the center of the leaf looks a little messy, make 2 or more passes going up the penciled vein line. This will help camouflage the irregularities that occur.

5. Press using steam after completing each leaf or when you move the hoop.

Remember to put an additional strip of tear-away stabilizer under the stem area. This keeps the area stable and reduces puckering.

TIP

6. Repeat Steps 2–5 until all the leaf shapes are embroidered. When traveling from one leaf to another, you may stitch up and down the pencil stem and vein lines instead of starting and stopping.

7. Thread the machine with the stem color thread. Place the 2″ × 7″ rectangle of tear-away stabilizer under the stem area of the project and secure in the embroidery hoop.

8. Begin at one end of the drawn stem and stitch the main stem 2–8 times. Create tiny stems that hold the leaves onto the branch by stitching to the base of the leaf and back 1 or 2 times.

9. Remove the embroidered project from the hoop. Press using steam.

Finish

See pages 56–57 for a complete description of finishing techniques.

1. Pin the embroidered project onto an ironing board or dressmaker's board so that it is perfectly square. Steam the project heavily with an iron and let it cool. Make sure it is completely dry before removing it from the board. If you started with a 9½″ block, try to steam it until it is the same size again.

2. Remove excess nylon net or tear-away stabilizer.

3. Layer and quilt the project.

4. Block your quilt.

5. Square up and trim to 9″ × 9″.

6. Bind.

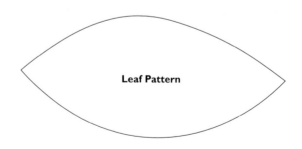

Leaf Pattern

THE PATCHWORK HEART, 8¹/₂″ × 8¹/₂″

PATCHWORK HEART

This charming heart is a simple shape to fill with zigzag free-motion embroidery.

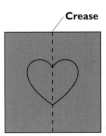

SUPPLIES

See pages 26–40 for a complete description of supplies.

FABRIC

- 1 square 9˝ × 9˝ (or larger) of solid or mottled fabric for the background
- 1 square 5˝ × 5˝ of red fabric for the heart
- Fabric for the binding and backing
- Batting

THREAD

- 40-weight decorative thread: solid or variegated, in yellow, red, and blue for the heart
- Bobbin thread

STABILIZERS

- 1 square 8˝ × 8˝ of nonwoven interfacing, nylon net, or water-soluble stabilizer as a stabilizer
- 1 square 6˝ × 6˝ of paper-back fusible web

INSTRUCTIONS

Prepare the Appliqué

See pages 30–32 for a complete description of fusing techniques.

1. Trace the heart onto paper-backed fusible web and fuse it to the wrong side of the red heart fabric. Use the heart pattern on page 73.

2. Cut out the heart and remove the paper backing.

3. Use the heart pattern as a guide, and draw lines on the right side of the fabric to divide the heart into 4 segments for the embroidery.

4. Fold the heart and the background square in half vertically and finger-press.

5. Line up the creases, centering the heart on the background square. Press in place using steam.

Center heart and press using steam.

Embroider

See pages 52–53 for a complete description of zigzag free-motion techniques.

1. Place the prepared project on top of your choice of stabilizer and secure in an embroidery hoop.

2. Use a darning foot. Lower the feed dogs and thread the machine with yellow thread. If you have the needle up/down option on the machine, set the needle in the down position.

3. Set the machine for a medium-width zigzag stitch. Zigzag free-motion really distorts the fabric. Using both the stabilizer and hoop together will help keep the project from curling up.

4. Begin stitching at the edge of the heart and move in the direction indicated by the arrows on the pattern until you reach the drawn line. Shift the heart slightly to the left and stitch back to the edge of the heart. Continue in this manner until the entire section is filled with thread.

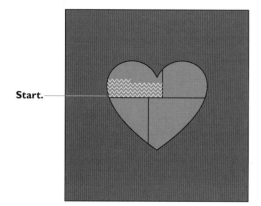

Stitch from edge to drawn line.

Pivot and stitch in opposite direction.

6. Repeat Steps 4 and 5 for the remaining 3 sections, changing thread color each time. Secure the ends as described on page 54. By changing the direction of the stitching with each change of thread color, you will create the appearance of a Four-Patch heart.

7. Remove the embroidered project from the hoop. Press using steam.

Finish

See pages 56–57 for a complete description of the finishing techniques.

1. Pin the embroidered project onto an ironing board or dressmaker's board so that it is perfectly square. Steam the project heavily with an iron and let it cool. Make sure it is completely dry before removing it from the board. If you started with a 9˝ block, try to steam it until it is the same size again.

2. Remove excess nylon net or tear-away stabilizer.

3. Layer and quilt.

4. Block your quilt.

5. Square up and trim to 8½˝ × 8½˝.

6. Bind.

TIP

If the fabric is puckering too much under the stress of the zigzag stitching, loosen the tension. Continue to loosen it, one number at a time, until the puckering is reduced.

5. Pivot the project and stitch in the opposite direction, covering the section with a second layer of thread. Changing the direction helps to completely fill up the area.

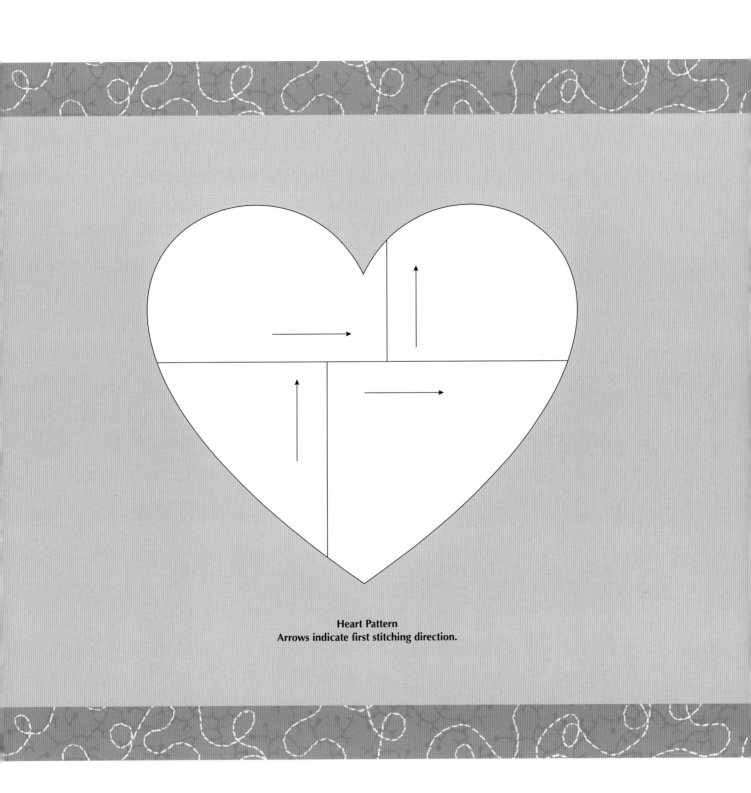

Heart Pattern
Arrows indicate first stitching direction.

Photo by Sharron Risedorph

BUTTON FLOWERS, 9″ × 9″

BUTTON FLOWERS

These flowers will give you practice blending colors to sculpt a round object using a free-motion zigzag stitch.

SUPPLIES

See pages 26–40 for a complete description of supplies.

FABRIC

- 1 square 6″ × 6″ of a solid or mottled fabric for the center

- 2 squares 6″ × 6″ of a coordinating fabric for the corners

- 3 circles 2″ in diameter of gold fabric for the flower centers

- 3 circles 3″ in diameter of yellow fabric for the outer petals

- 1 rectangle 3″ × 7″ of green fabric for the leaves

- Fabric for the backing and binding

- Batting

THREAD

- Thread to match the background for piecing

- 40-weight decorative thread: 5 colors ranging from yellow to deep gold for the flowers

- 40-weight green variegated thread for the leaves

- Bobbin thread

STABILIZERS

- 1 square 8″ × 8″ of nonwoven interfacing, nylon net, or water-soluble stabilizer as a stabilizer

- 1 rectangle 3″ × 6″ of tear-away stabilizer for stems

- 1 square 12″ × 12″ of paper-backed fusible web

INSTRUCTIONS

Make the Background

1. Cut both corner squares diagonally once to create 4 triangles.

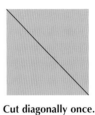

Cut diagonally once.

2. Center the long diagonal side of 2 triangles on opposite sides of the center square, right sides together. Sew using a ¼″ seam.

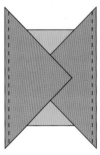

Sew triangles to opposite sides of center square.

3. Press the seams toward the corner triangles.

4. Attach 2 more triangles on the remaining sides. Press.

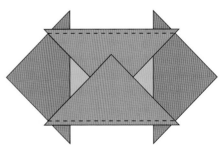

Sew remaining triangles to opposite sides.

Prepare the Appliqué

See pages 30–32 for a complete description of fusing techniques.

1. Trace the flowers, flower centers, and leaf shapes onto paper-backed fusible web and fuse to the wrong side of your fabrics. Use the button flower pattern on the next page.

2. Cut out the shapes and remove the paper backing.

3. Arrange the flowers, flower centers, and leaves on the pieced background.

4. Press in place using steam.

5. Use the button flower pattern and lightly mark with a pencil the position of the 3 flower stems, letting them curve slightly. Draw veins in the leaves.

6. Decide which direction the light is coming from. Use a pencil to divide the flower centers into shading units.

Divide flower centers into shading units.

Embroider

1. Place the prepared project over your choice of stabilizer and secure in an embroidery hoop. Lower the feed dogs, thread the machine with the green variegated thread, and set for straight stitch.

2. Begin at one end of a vein and stitch 1–2 times. Repeat for each vein.

3. Start at the edge of a leaf section and move the fabric slowly back and forth, covering the entire section. Make sure the stitching line goes completely over the outside edge of the leaf. Secure the ends as discussed on page 54.

Start.

Begin on outside edge, covering each section with curved stitching lines.

4. Repeat for the remaining 2 leaves.

5. Remove the project from the hoop and press using steam. Let cool.

6. Rehoop and thread the machine with yellow thread.

7. Start at the edge of a petal section and move the fabric slowly back and forth, covering the outer yellow petals. Secure the ends. Leave the gold flower center empty.

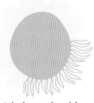

Stitch petals with yellow thread.

8. Repeat for the remaining 2 flowers.

Fill the Centers

When you first see this project up close you may be disappointed with the shaded centers. Stand back—a three-dimensional effect is what you want here. This is an easy way to make any circular object appear to be a ball. The ornaments on a Christmas tree could also be done this way.

See pages 52–53 for a complete description of zigzag free-motion techniques.

1. Choose 3 or 4 shades of decorative thread, from yellow to dark gold, for the centers.

2. Set the machine for medium-width zigzag stitch.

3. Start with the lightest yellow/gold for the small oval off-center. Fill the center, stitching in one direction and then going over it again in the opposite direction. Make it dense in the center and lighter on the edges so it will blend with the next layers of thread. Secure the ends.

Fill the center, stitching in both directions.

4. With the next darker thread, fill in the next segment on the shady side of the center, overlapping the stitching on the edges of the first section. Overlapping creates a subtle blending of the colors.

5. Continue filling each successive segment with darker thread until the center is completely covered.

6. Repeat Steps 3–5 for the remaining 2 flower centers.

7. Remove the project from the hoop and press using steam. Let cool.

Stems

1. It is important to have 2 layers of a crisp tear-away stabilizer under the area for the stems. Place the 3″ × 6″ rectangle of tear-away stabilizer, folded in half, under the stem area and rehoop the project.

2. Thread the machine with green variegated thread and set the machine for straight stitch.

3. Begin at one end of the drawn stem and stitch, going back and forth at least 4 times to create a heavy line. Secure the ends.

4. Repeat for the remaining 2 stems.

5. Remove the embroidered project from the hoop. Press using steam.

Finish

See pages 56–57 for a complete description of finishing techniques.

1. Pin the embroidered project onto an ironing board or dressmaker's board so that it is perfectly square. Steam the project heavily with an iron and let it cool. Make sure it is completely dry before removing it from the board. If you started with a 9½″ block, try to steam it until it is the same size again.

2. Remove excess nylon net or tear-away stabilizer.

3. Layer and quilt.

4. Block your quilt.

5. Square up and trim to 9″ × 9″.

6. Bind.

Button Flower Pattern

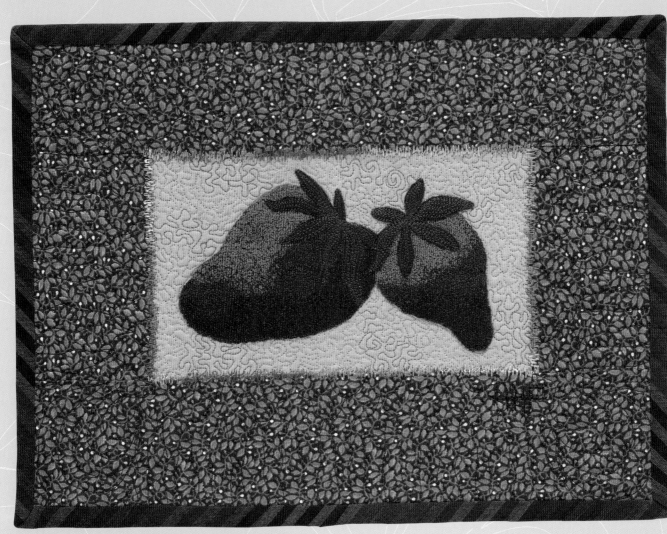

Photo by Sharon Risedorph

STRAWBERRIES, 11^1/$_2$″ × 8^1/$_2$″

STRAWBERRY CIRCLES

These strawberries are a tasteful way to practice free-motion circular stitching. This stitch takes time to fill up an area, but the pebbly texture is worth it.

SUPPLIES

See pages 26–40 for a complete description of supplies.

FABRIC

- 1 rectangle 7½″ × 4½″ of light green for the background
- 1 strip 3″ × 37″ of a darker green for the border
- 1 rectangle 3″ × 7½″ of red for the strawberries
- 1 square 4″ × 4″ of dark green for the strawberry tops
- Fabric for the backing and binding
- Batting

THREAD

- 40-weight decorative thread: 3 red colors that will blend for the strawberries
- 40-weight decorative thread: green for the strawberry tops
- Bobbin thread: 1 red and 1 green
- 40-weight variegated thread: green for inner border (optional)

STABILIZERS

- 1 rectangle 5″ × 8″ of tear-away stabilizer, nonwoven interfacing, or water-soluble stabilizer as a stabilizer
- 1 strip 1″ × 24″ of tear-away stabilizer
- 1 rectangle 3″ × 7½″ of paper-backed fusible web

INSTRUCTIONS

Make the Background

1. From the border fabric cut 2 strips 3″ × 4½″ and 2 strips 3″ × 12½″.

2. Sew the 3″ × 4½″ strips to opposite (short) ends of the light green background using a ¼″ seam.

3. Press the seams toward the border.

4. Sew the 3″ × 12½″ strips to opposite (long) sides of the background. Press.

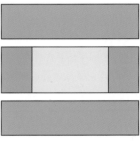

Assemble background.

5. Optional detail: before fusing the strawberries and tops in place, I like to make a line of decorative stitching (with the feed dogs up) on the outer seam of the light green center, with variegated thread. Use the decorative stitch of your choice. Place the 1″-wide strip of stabilizer under the seam and stitch right on the seam itself. This adds an interesting detail to the finished piece.

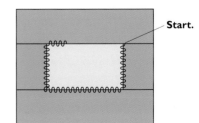

Optional decorative stitching

Prepare the Appliqué

See pages 30–32 for a complete description of fusing techniques.

1. Trace the strawberries and tops onto paper-backed fusible web and fuse to the wrong side of the red and green fabric. Be sure to trace the shading lines of the berries. Use the strawberry patterns on the next page.

2. Cut out the shapes and remove the paper backing.

3. Place the berries on the prepared background so they slightly overlap.

4. Press in place using steam.

5. With a pencil, lightly draw the shading lines as shown on the pattern piece.

6. Cut out the strawberry tops exactly on the lines and remove the paper backing.

7. Place the tops on the berries so they slightly overlap. Press in place using steam.

Embroider

See pages 47–49 for a complete description of free-motion embroidery techniques.

1. Place the prepared project on top of your choice of stabilizer and secure in an embroidery hoop, with one strawberry centered in the hoop. Lower the feed dogs, thread the machine with the lightest red thread, and set the machine for straight stitch.

2. Begin stitching the top section of the strawberry, making tiny circles about the size of the head of a pin or nail. This seems small, but this is what creates the interesting texture. Continue to move the embroidery slowly around and around in one place until the circle is filled with thread. Now move over and start another circle. Continue making little circles until the whole section is filled up with thread. This is a time-consuming process. Secure the ends as discussed on page 54.

Go around each little circle 3 or 4 times until covered with thread.

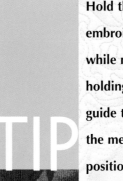

Hold the plastic edge of the embroidery hoop with 2 hands while making tiny circles. Avoid holding the metal handles to help guide the fabric. This might cause the metal clamp to snap out of position.

3. Thread the machine with the next darker red.

4. Repeat Step 2, filling the middle section of the berry. To blend the darker red with the neighboring lighter section, stitch around the outside of some of the lighter circles where the two colors meet. Continue outlining some of the circles until there is no longer an obvious line between the two colors. There aren't any rules about how much stitching needs to be done. Continue to stitch, overlap, and blend the sections until you are pleased with the appearance. Secure the ends.

Start here.

To blend two different colors, with the darker shade make small **open** circles or loops around the lighter red circles. Continue making these circles or loops until one color appears to melt into the other.

5. Thread the machine with the darkest red thread. Repeat Steps 2 and 4, filling the last section of the berry. Take care to blend where the two colors meet. Secure the ends.

6. Thread the machine with the green thread.

7. Stitch the tops using a straight stitch, going back and forth until the little leaves are full of green thread. Make sure the stitching line goes completely over the edge of the leaf. Secure the ends.

Stitch green tops with straight stitch.

8. Remove the project from the hoop and press using steam. Let cool.

9. Rehoop the project, centering the second strawberry. Repeat Steps 2–7 for the second strawberry.

10. Remove the project from the hoop. Press using steam.

Finish

See pages 56–57 for a complete description of finishing techniques.

1. Pin the embroidered project onto an ironing board or dressmaker's board so that it is perfectly square. Steam the project heavily with an iron and let it cool. Make sure it is completely dry before removing it from the board. If you started with a 12½″ × 9½″ block, try to steam it until it is the same size again.

2. Remove excess nylon net or tear-away stabilizer.

3. Layer and quilt.

4. Block your quilt.

5. Square up and trim to 11½″ × 8½″.

6. Bind.

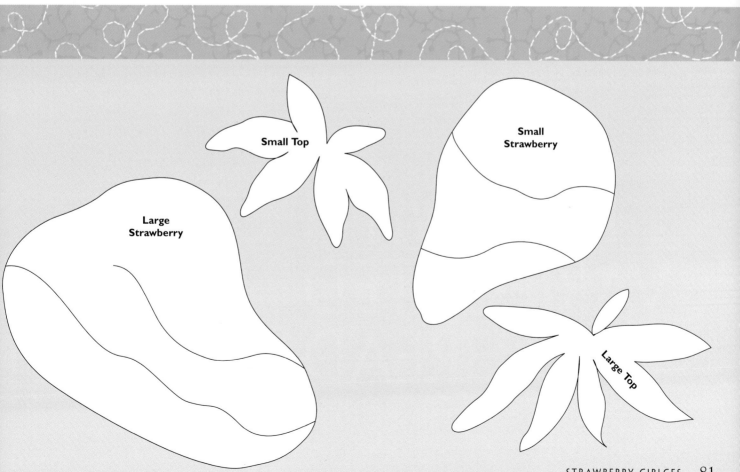

Small Top

Small Strawberry

Large Strawberry

Large Top

Photo by Sharon Risedorph

VARIEGATED FLOWERS, 12½″ × 12½″

FUN WITH VARIEGATED THREAD

These flowers, stems, and leaves are all stitched with the same spool of variegated thread. Choose your favorite spool of thread to embroider this project!

SUPPLIES

See pages 26–40 for a complete description of supplies.

FABRIC

- 1 rectangle 13″ × 4″ of medium green for the grass
- 1 rectangle 13″ × 9½″ of light blue for the sky
- 1 rectangle 6″ × 12″ of dark green for the leaves and stems
- 3 squares 4½″ × 4½″ of a different color fabric each, to match the variegated thread
- Fabric for the backing and binding
- Batting

THREAD

- Thread to match the background for piecing
- 40-weight variegated thread: a minimum of 3–5 colors
- Bobbin thread to blend with the variegated thread (I used green.)

STABILIZERS

- 1 square 13″ × 13″ of nonwoven interfacing, tear-away stabilizer, or nylon net as a stabilizer
- 1 square 15″ × 15″ of paper-backed fusible web

INSTRUCTIONS

Make the Background

1. Sew the long side of the light-blue sky fabric to the long side of the grass fabric using a ¼″ seam.

2. Press the seam toward the green fabric.

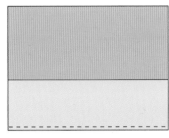

Sew using ¹⁄₄″ seam.

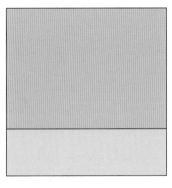

Press.

Prepare the Appliqué

See pages 30–32 for a complete description of fusing techniques.

1. Cut a 2″ × 7″ rectangle on the crosswise grain from the dark green fabric and set it aside for stems.

2. Trace the flower and leaf shapes onto the paper-backed fusible web and fuse to the wrong side of the fabrics. Use the patterns on page 85.

3. Cut out the shapes and remove the paper backing.

4. Arrange the flowers on the background, letting them overlap. (Use the photo on page 82 for reference.)

5. Arrange the leaves on the background, creating a center where the sky meets the grass.

6. Cut a 2″ × 7″ strip of paper-backed fusible web. Fuse to the back of the fabric for the stems.

7. Cut 3 stems from the fused fabric, each about ¼″–½″ wide. Cut them with a slight curve. Trim the ends of the stems into a gradual point.

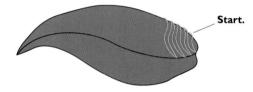

Slight curve and gradual points create natural appearance.

8. Tuck one end of each stem under a flower and place the other end at the center of the leaves. Trim excess fabric, retaining a gradual point.

9. Press all the pieces in place using steam.

10. Use the flower pattern and lightly mark with a pencil the position where the flower cone meets the petals.

11. Use a pencil to draw the center vein in the middle of each leaf.

12. Put a straight pin on either end of each leaf, right where the seam goes under it. From the wrong side, trim the seam away between the pins to reduce bulk. (See page 47 for more on trimming seam allowances.)

Embroider

See pages 47–49 for a complete description of free-motion embroidery techniques.

1. Place the prepared project on top of your choice of stabilizer and secure in an embroidery hoop. Lower the feed dogs, thread the machine with the variegated thread, and set the machine for straight stitch.

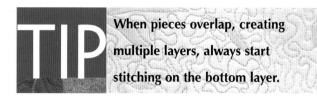

TIP When pieces overlap, creating multiple layers, always start stitching on the bottom layer.

2. Begin with the leaf that is tucked under the other leaves and flowers. Start at the base of the leaf and move the fabric slowly back and forth, covering the leaf from the drawn center vein to the outside edge. Make sure the stitching line goes completely over the edge of the leaf. Move up the side toward the leaf tip, allowing the stitching line to curve, then turn around and move down the remaining half of the leaf. Secure the ends as discussed on page 54.

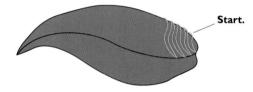

Start at base, allowing stitching line to curve.

3. Remove the project from the hoop and press with steam. Let cool.

4. Rehoop. Embroider the stems of the flowers. I find short diagonal lines moving up the stem easier to do than long straight ones; the final result is also more pleasing. Secure the ends. Remove the project from the hoop and press with steam after each stem is embroidered. Let cool.

5. Embroider the flowers in the same sequence, from bottom layer to top. In this example the order is blue, yellow, red. Embroider the petals first, moving up and down the length of each petal. Move to the center cone next, stitching back and forth following the center curve. Finish the cone with a little spiral at the tip. Secure the ends. Remove the project from the hoop and press with steam after each flower is embroidered. Let cool.

6. Remove the embroidered project from the hoop. Press using steam.

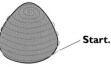

Stitch center cone.

Finish

See pages 56–57 for a complete description of finishing techniques.

1. Pin the embroidered project onto an ironing board or dressmaker's board so that it is perfectly square. Steam the project heavily with an iron and let it cool. Make sure it is completely dry before removing it from the board. If you started with a 13″ block, try to steam it until it is the same size again.

2. Remove excess nylon net or tear-away stabilizer.

3. Layer and quilt.

4. Block your quilt.

5. Square up and trim to 12½″ × 12½″.

6. Bind.

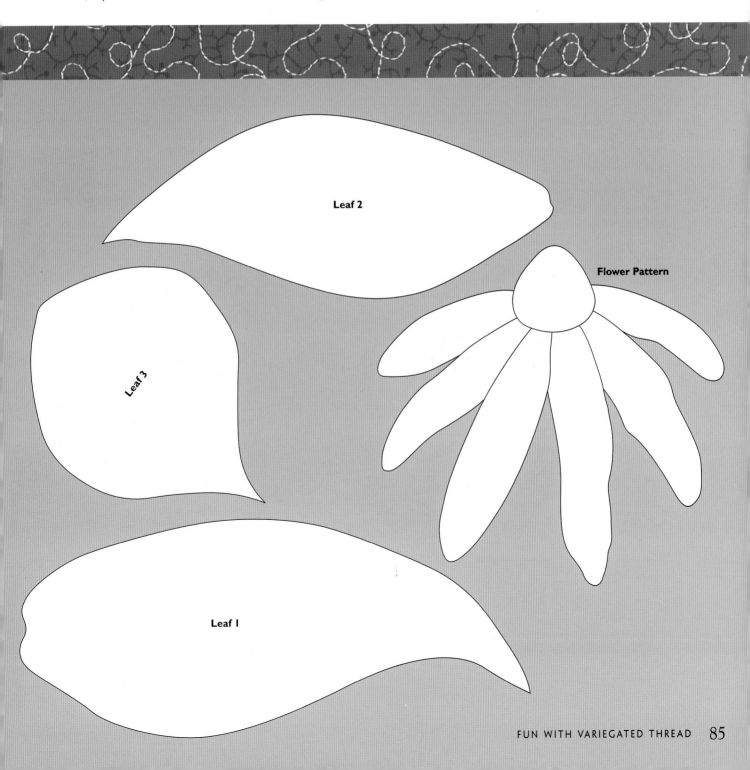

Leaf 2

Flower Pattern

Leaf 3

Leaf 1

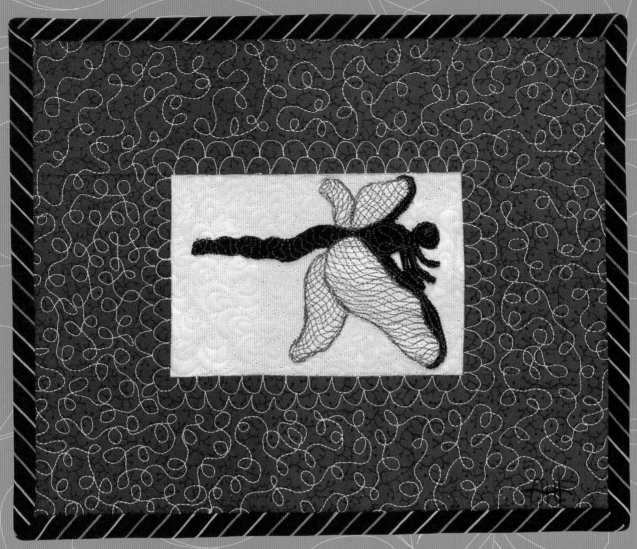

DRAGONFLY, 10˝ X 8˝

DRAGONFLY WITH METALLIC THREAD

This shimmering dragonfly was made using a dark solid rayon thread on the body, a flat red metallic for highlighting the body, and a twisted red metallic and flat iridescent clear metallic on the wings.

SUPPLIES

See pages 26–40 for a complete description of supplies.

FABRIC

- 1 rectangle 4″ × 5½″ of yellow fabric for the background

- 1 strip 3″ × 32″ of red fabric for the border

- 1 square 4″ × 4″ of fabric for the wings (This can match the background if you wish.)

- 1 rectangle 4″ × 5″ of dark fabric for the body

- Fabric for the backing and binding

- Batting

THREAD

- Thread to match the background for piecing

- 30- or 40-weight decorative thread to match the body fabric

- Flat metallic thread: 1 red for the body and 1 clear iridescent for the wings

- Twisted red metallic thread for the wings

- Bobbin thread

STABILIZERS

- 2 rectangles 4″ × 5½″ of tear-away stabilizer for the body

- 1 rectangle 4″ × 5½″ of water-soluble stabilizer or nonwoven interfacing as stabilizer for the wings

- 1 rectangle 4″ × 5″ of paper-backed fusible web

INSTRUCTIONS

Make the Background

1. From the border fabric strip cut 2 strips 3″ × 4″ and 2 strips 3″ × 10½″.

2. Sew the 3″ × 4″ strips to opposite (short) ends of the yellow background using a ¼″ seam.

3. Press the seams toward the border.

4. Sew the 3″ × 10½″ strips to opposite (long) sides of the background. Press.

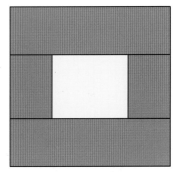

Assemble background.

Prepare the Appliqué

See pages 30–32 for a complete description of fusing techniques.

1. Trace the body of the dragonfly onto paper-backed fusible web and fuse to the wrong side of the body fabric. Use the dragonfly pattern on page 90.

2. Cut out and remove the paper backing.

3. Center and place the body on the background. Do *not* press yet!

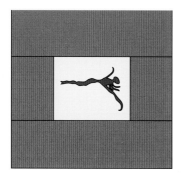

Center and place body.

4. Trace the wings of the dragonfly onto paper-backed fusible web and fuse to the wrong side of the wing fabric.

5. Cut out and remove the paper backing.

6. Place the wings on the body, taking care to tuck the edges of the wings under the body.

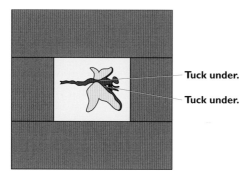

Tuck under.
Tuck under.

Tuck edges of wings under body.

7. Press in place using steam. Turn over and press again.

Embroider

See pages 47–49 for a complete description of free-motion embroidery techniques.

See pages 35 and 55 for specific information on metallic thread.

Embroider the Body

The long body of the dragonfly is segmented, and the embroidery will try to imitate this. Small circles up the length of the body will give a segmented appearance.

1. Secure the project in the embroidery hoop. Pin 2 layers of tear-away stabilizer under the dragonfly.

2. Lower the feed dogs, thread the machine with the decorative thread for the body, and set the machine for straight stitch.

3. Make small circles, filling them with thread before moving on to the next area. The circles will be a little smaller than a dime. Take care *not* to stitch the body where the wings attach.

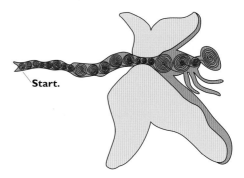

Start.

Stitch small circles filled with thread to cover body.

4. Detail the legs and forward edge of the wings with a few rows of a straight stitch.

5. Make sure the body is filled with thread. Go back and fill any empty areas.

6. Secure the ends as discussed on page 54.

7. The body may have lots of little frayed edges. Fold the fabric so the frayed edge stands straight up and trim away all the little threads now. (See page 58 for more on cleaning up the edges.)

8. Press using steam.

Embroider the Body With Metallic Thread

1. Secure the project in the embroidery hoop. Be sure you have the correct needle for metallic thread. Thread the machine with the flat red metallic thread.

2. Lightly detail the body with open circles. Stitch over the wings, head, and legs one time. This stitching will add highlights and a little glitter.

3. Remove the tear-away stabilizer.

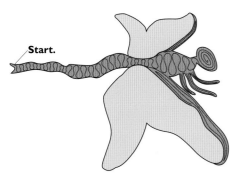

Flat red metallic thread adds highlights.

Embroider the Wings

1. Rehoop the project, placing the wing area on top of your choice of stabilizer.

2. Use twisted red metallic thread to outline the wing shape 1 or 2 times. This will define the shape for you. Make sure you include the section on the body where the wing joins.

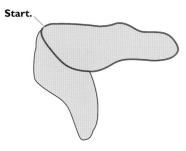

Outline wing with metallic thread.

3. To create the effect of delicate wings, stitch wavy lines at an angle about ⅛″ apart.

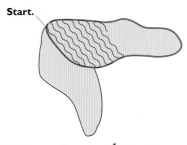

Stitch wavy lines about ⅛″ apart.

4. When the wing is filled in one direction, finish filling in by sewing in the opposite direction.

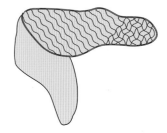

Repeat, sewing in opposite direction.

5. After going back and forth so many times, the edges of the wings will look ragged. Cover this up by going around the outside of the wing again with the same metallic thread 1 or 2 more times.

6. Repeat Steps 1–5 for the remaining 3 wings.

7. Remove from the hoop. Use a pressing cloth to protect the metallic threads and press using steam. Turn over and press again.

8. If you would like more glitz, you can add a layer of clear iridescent metallic thread on the wings. Stitch only every 1 or 2 lines to lightly fill the network. Stitch in just one direction in each wing, taking care not to stitch over the iridescent thread, as it can break if pierced with a needle. Treat this thread delicately!

9. Use a pressing cloth and press using steam.

TIP When quilting, take care to avoid stitching over the flat metallic thread. Quilt on either side of the stitching so it doesn't break the thread.

Finish

See pages 56–57 for a complete description of finishing techniques.

1. Pin the embroidered project onto an ironing board or dressmaker's board so that it is perfectly square. Steam the project heavily with an iron and let it cool. Make sure it is completely dry before removing it from the board. If you started with an 10½˝ × 9˝ block, try to steam it until it is the same size again.

2. Remove excess nylon net or tear-away stabilizer.

3. Layer and quilt.

4. Block your quilt.

5. Square up and trim to 10˝ × 8˝.

6. Bind.

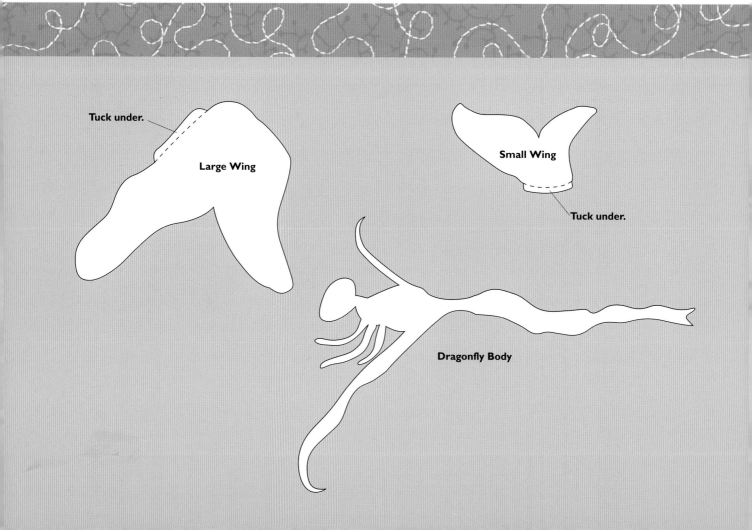

Tuck under.

Large Wing

Small Wing

Tuck under.

Dragonfly Body

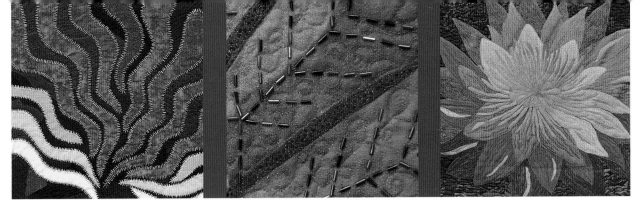

TROUBLESHOOTING GUIDE TO THREAD WORK

The best way to handle problems is to understand what causes them. There are three basic reasons for stitching problems: **tension, stitch balance,** and **friction**. This part of the book may lack color and excitement, but this chapter *will* help solve your stitching problems!

TENSION

Indications of Tension Problems

If the tension on top is too tight, the following problems occur:

- The bobbin thread is pulled up to the surface.

- The top thread appears to be just lying on the surface of the work, and actual stitches are not well defined.

If the tension on top is too loose, the following problems occur:

- Loops of top thread show on the underside.

- Thread makes loops on the top side, or you can pull the stitches loose with your fingers.

If the bobbin tension is too tight, the following problems occur:

- The bobbin thread appears to just lie on the surface, and stitches are not defined on the underside.

- The top thread is pulled to the back and little bits of top color are visible in between stitches.

If the bobbin tension is too loose, the following problems occur:

- Loops of bobbin thread are visible on top.

- The bobbin thread will pull up and be quite visible when the direction of stitching is changed and at the end of the line of stitching.

- You can pull the stitches loose with your fingers.

Solving Tension Problems

If the problem is tension related, re-thread the machine, making sure the presser foot is up. If you still have a tension problem, adjust the top tension first. Finally, if necessary, adjust the bobbin tension. (See page 42 for more on adjusting the bobbin tension.)

BALANCE

A balanced stitch is one in which the top and bottom threads have equal tension. When doing decorative thread work, the types of thread chosen for top and bottom are often not the same weight.

Indications of Balance Problems

■ Peek-through—usually the heavier thread pulls the lighter-weight thread toward its side.

Solving Balance Problems

■ Tighten the tension on the side that has the lighter-weight thread.

■ Loosen the tension on the side with the heavier thread.

■ Change the color of the bobbin thread so it blends with the top thread, so there is less peek-through.

■ Change the type of thread used in the bobbin, so the weight is similar to the thread used in the top.

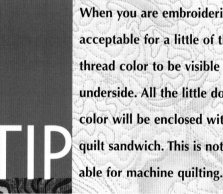

TIP When you are embroidering, it is acceptable for a little of the top thread color to be visible on the underside. All the little dots of color will be enclosed within the quilt sandwich. This is not acceptable for machine quilting.

FRICTION

Indications of Friction Problems

■ Thread frays and shreds.

Solving Friction Problems

■ Use a larger size needle or loosen the tension.

■ As a last resort, lubricate the thread with silicone product. *Please check with your machine dealer to make sure this is acceptable to use on your brand.*

UNDERSTANDING THE PROBLEM

Now that you have a greater understanding of the major sources of free-motion embroidery problems, you will find it easier to diagnose what is happening with your sewing machine. When troubles strike, I always advise that you take a break from the sewing machine for a few minutes. Rest your eyes and do something else before returning to the machine to solve your problem. Go through the possibilities in the same order as listed above. Is it a tension problem? Are the threads not balanced? Or is friction causing the thread to shred or break? **Following is a list of common problems and solutions.**

PROBLEM	SOLUTIONS
Skipped stitches	■ Replace the needle. ■ Use a silicone product on the thread. ■ Trim out excess seam allowances where possible to reduce bulk. ■ Stitch more slowly.
Shredding top thread	■ Re-thread the machine. ■ Loosen the top tension. ■ Use the next size larger needle (especially if the fabric is tightly woven or is printed with white or metallic gold paint). ■ Select a top-stitch or embroidery-type needle. ■ Try a new needle. ■ Skip the last thread guide above the needle.
Breaking thread	■ Re-thread the machine. ■ Loosen the top tension. ■ Replace the needle. ■ The top spool of thread is spinning too fast and the thread winds around the spool pin; use plastic caps or felt pads, as directed by the owner's manual. ■ Thread catches on the bottom of the almost empty spool as it unwinds; turn the spool around or wind the remaining thread on a bobbin and place it on the spool pin. ■ Thread catches on the notch or a rough spot on the edge of a spool; smooth with a nail file or emery board. ■ Check the hole in the throat plate for a rough spot or burr. Smooth it with a metal file or take it in for repair or replacement. ■ Have someone watch you sew until the thread breaks again; he or she may be better able to see what is happening.
Thread snarling or knotting in or around tension guides	■ Use a thread net. ■ Switch the spool from horizontal to vertical, or the reverse. ■ Use a thread stand. ■ Turn the spool around.
Needle breaking	■ You are stitching through too many layers of fabric; trim out excess. ■ The spool is spinning too fast and thread is winding around the pin; use a spool cap, felt pad, thread stand, or thread net.
Difficulty in winding bobbin	■ Insert the thread through the little hole or slot in the bobbin and place the bobbin on the bobbin winder. Hold the end of the thread with your hand and begin winding the bobbin. When there is enough thread to hold the end in place, clip off the end.
Fused shapes starting to peel up on quilt top	■ Steam press for 10 seconds to reactivate the fusible web. Resteam as needed.
Difficulty removing thread from machine	■ Lift the presser foot to reduce the tension or pressure on the upper thread before pulling the thread out.
Top thread tangling	■ Change the position of the spool to horizontal or vertical. ■ Turn the spool around. ■ Use a thread stand. ■ Tighten the top tension. ■ Use a thread net.

PROBLEM	SOLUTIONS
Bobbin thread showing on top	■ Remove the bobbin from the machine, then return it to the bobbin case. ■ Tighten the bobbin tension. ■ Loosen the top tension. ■ Use a different type of bobbin thread. ■ Use a different color of bobbin thread. ■ Use a new bobbin.
Loops of top thread showing on bottom between each stitch	■ Re-thread the machine, making sure the presser foot is up. ■ Tighten the top tension.
Irregular loops or tangles on underside	■ Try all the above options. ■ Take the machine in for repair of a possible burr in the bobbin case or in the hole of the throat plate.
Quilt top dragging or pulling while sewing; difficulty moving it under the needle	■ Clip all loose thread on the back. ■ Turn your work in a different direction. ■ Gently lift up a corner or one edge of the hoop so that it doesn't catch on the front edge of the throat plate. ■ Fold or roll up excess quilt top so it is easier to move or guide. ■ Use furniture polish on the bed of the table and the machine. Make sure it is dry and excess is removed before you resume sewing. ■ Reduce the amount of pressure on the presser foot. (This knob is usually found on the top or side of the machine. Not all machines have this adjustment.) ■ Pfaff owners, make sure the presser foot is lowered only halfway; there is a notch midway between the up and down positions (also known as the embroidery/darning position).
Iron sticking to the top of heavily stitched areas	■ Use a pressing cloth for heat-sensitive thread and to prevent fabric scorching. ■ Before pressing directly onto thread, always test a sample first. ■ Clean the soleplate by using a commercial cleaner or by putting cotton fabric or batting on the edge of the ironing surface and pulling the hot iron slowly across the edge 5–10 times until the black residue is removed.
Needle catching or causing snags on fabric	■ Throw away the needle and put in a new one.
Nothing seems to work right on the sewing machine	■ Turn off the power for 10 seconds to let the computer in the machine reset itself. ■ Check the power supply. If you are using a power strip or surge protector, plug the machine directly into the wall outlet. ■ Try a different spool of thread. ■ Replace the fuse in the power strip. ■ Re-thread the machine, making sure the presser foot is up. ■ Take the bobbin out and make sure it is not in backward and therefore unwinding in the incorrect direction. ■ Use the same decorative thread on the top and in the bobbin. ■ Give up for the day; have a cup of tea and a cookie. ■ Take the machine in for servicing.

INDEX

ABOUT THE AUTHOR

Photo by Marco D. Black of Signature Studios, Racine, WI

Ann Fahl took a beginning quilting class in 1978 and completed her first quilt—a gift for her mother. Everything about making quilts appealed to her; she liked to sew, loved color and fabric, and loved creating her own designs. The rest is history. She has been making original quilts ever since.

Ann has worked to create original designs with the highest possible level of workmanship. Many of her quilts have won awards at quilt competitions across the country. They can be found in private and corporate collections across the United States. Pictures of her quilts are in books and periodicals as well as on her website, www.AnnFahl.com. Ann teaches quilting, has a line of patterns, and occasionally writes for quilt publications.

Ann has a degree in textiles and clothing from the University of Wisconsin. Working in a studio at home, she has managed to balance a career in quilting with time with her husband, raising two sons, a cat, gardening, and a new hobby of genealogy.

RESOURCES

ONLINE RESOURCES

Thread and Sewing Supplies

Madeira Thread www.madeirausa.com

Mettler Thread www.arova-mettler.com

Sulky Thread www.sulky.com

Superior Threads www.superiorthreads.com

Web of Thread www.webofthread.com

Tools

Janome Sewing Machines www.janome.com

Gingher Scissors www.gingher.com

OTT-LITE Technology www.ottlite.com

Schmetz Sewing Machine Needles www.schmetz.com

Information on Sewing Machines

Sussex Sewing Machines www.sussexsewingmachines.com

Brother Sewing Machines www.brothersews.com

Quilter's Gloves

Timid Thimble Creations www.timidthimble.com

HELPFUL BOOKS

All About Machine Arts—Decorative Techniques From A to Z, by *Sew News, Creative Machine Embroidery,* and C&T Publishing

All About Quilting From A to Z, by *Quilter's Newsletter Magazine, Quiltmaker,* and C&T Publishing

Guide to Machine Quilting, by Diane Gaudynski

Heirloom Machine Quilting, 4th Edition, by Harriet Hargrave

Show Me How to Machine Quilt, by Kathy Sandbach

Thread Magic: The Enchanted World of Ellen Anne Eddy, by Ellen Anne Eddy

Threadplay With Libby Lehman, by Libby Lehman

QUILTING SUPPLIES

Cotton Patch Mail Order
3405 Hall Lane, Dept. CTB
Lafayette, CA 94595
(800) 835-4418
(925) 283-7883
email: quiltusa@yahoo.com
website: www.quiltusa.com

Note: Fabrics used in the quilts shown may not be currently available since fabric manufacturers keep most fabrics in print for only a short time.

For more information, write for a free catalog:
C&T Publishing, Inc.
P.O. Box 1456
Lafayette, CA 94549
(800) 284-1114
email: ctinfo@ctpub.com
website: www.ctpub.com